A POCKETFUL

OF POEMS

VINTAGE

VERSE

DAVID MADDEN

Louisiana State University

HARCOURT BRACE COLLEGE PUBLISHERS

Fort Worth   Philadelphia   San Diego   New York   Orlando   Austin   San Antonio
Toronto   Montreal   London   Sydney   Tokyo

Publisher	Ted Buchholz
Editor in Chief	Christopher P. Klein
Executive Editor	Michael A. Rosenberg
Assistant Editor	Tina Winslow
Project Editor	Laura J. Hanna
Art Directors	Melinda Welch/Nick Welch
Production Manager	Jane Tyndall Poncetti

ISBN: 0-15-502544-9
Library of Congress Catalog Card Number: 95-79366

Address for Domestic Orders
Harcourt College Publishers, 6277 Sea Harbor Drive, Orlando, FL 32887-6777
800-782-4479

Address for International Orders
International Customer Service
Harcourt, Inc., 6277 Sea Harbor Drive, Orlando, FL 32887-6777
407-345-3800
(fax) 407-345-4060
(e-mail) hbintl@harcourt.com

Address for Editorial Correspondence
Harcourt College Publishers, 301 Commerce Street, Suite 3700, Fort Worth, TX 76102

Web Site Address
http://www.harcourtcollege.com

Printed in the United States of America

0 1 2 3 4 5 6 7 8 9   039   16 15 14 13 12 11 10 9 8 7

Harcourt College Publishers

A Word from the Editor to Students and Teachers

You can actually afford this anthology. How does it feel in your hand? Companionable, I hope.

As with the two prose anthologies that launched the Pocketful series, *A Pocketful of Poems: Vintage Verse* is aimed at satisfying the need for a concise, quality collection that students will find inexpensive and that instructors will enjoy teaching.

The reception of this series has supported our original assumption that students and teachers would welcome an innovative alternative to huge anthologies, which are rarely used entirely, tend to be too bulky to carry and to handle in class, and are, above all, expensive.

A Pocketful of Poems contains 125 poems that research reveals to be currently among the most commonly studied in classes around the country.

The marginal notes on "Dover Beach" are intended to suggest ways to annotate all the other poems, providing a basis for class discussion, papers, and review for exams.

The design of the text encourages students to respond to the poems as they read. You will notice that the margins are wide enough to allow room for notes, questions, and student commentary.

Because there are many, varied approaches to the teaching of poetry, the alphabetical organization seems most useful. For the same reason, the supplementary material is limited to the marginal notes on "Dover Beach" and a list of "Questions that Give You Full Access to Each Poem."

At Harcourt Brace, my Acquisitions Editor, Michael Rosenberg, and my Assistant Editor, Tina Winslow, shared my vision of this text and supported my desire to try new approaches to the creation of textbooks. They helped shape the collection from start to finish. Thanks also to Project Editor Laura Hanna, Art Directors Melinda Welch and Nick Welch, and Production Manager, Jane Tyndall Ponceti, whose talents made it possible to meet the design and production challenges of the text.

We hope that students will find the cost refreshing and that the questions and annotations will help broaden their experience with the poems.

We are interested in hearing from you. To tell us your comments on how this text worked in your class, please respond in writing to Executive English Editor, Harcourt Brace, 301 Commerce Street, Suite 3700, Fort Worth, TX 76102.

David Madden
Louisiana State University

CONTENTS

Author	Title

Author	Title

Author	Title

Matthew Arnold (1822–1888)

Dover Beach 1867

The sea is calm tonight.
The tide is full, the moon lies fair
Upon the straits—on the French coast the light
Gleams and is gone; the cliffs of England stand,
5 Glimmering and vast, out in the tranquil bay.
Come to the window, sweet is the night air!
Only, from the long line of spray
Where the sea meets the moon-blanched land,
Listen! you hear the grating roar
10 Of pebbles which the waves draw back, and fling,
At their return, up the high strand,
Begin, and cease, and then again begin,
With tremulous cadence slow, and bring
The eternal note of sadness in.

15 Sophocles long ago
Heard it on the Aegean, and it brought
Into his mind the turbid ebb and flow
Of human misery; we
Find also in the sound a thought,
20 Hearing it by this distant northern sea.

The Sea of Faith
Was once, too, at the full, and round earth's shore
Lay like the folds of a bright girdle furled.
But now I only hear
25 Its melancholy, long, withdrawing roar,
Retreating, to the breath
Of the night wind, down the vast edges drear
And naked shingles° of the world.

Ah, love, let us be true
30 To one another! for the world, which seems
To lie before us like a land of dreams,
So various, so beautiful, so new,
Hath really neither joy, nor love, nor light,
Nor certitude, nor peace, nor help for pain;
35 And we are here as on a darkling plain
Swept with confused alarms of struggle and flight,
Where ignorant armies clash by night.

Possible Annotations on Second and Third Readings for Study, Discussion, Writing

Matthew Arnold

Dover Beach

TITLE: The setting

The sea is calm tonight.
The tide is full, the <u>moon</u> lies fair
Upon the straits—on the <u>French</u> coast the light
<u>G</u>leams and is gone; the cliffs of <u>England</u> stand,
5 <u>G</u>limmering and vast, out in the tranquil bay.
Come to the window, sweet is the night air!
Only, from <u>the long line of spray</u>
<u>Where the sea meets the moon-blanched land,</u>
Listen! you hear <u>the grating roar</u>
10 <u>Of pebbles</u> which the waves draw back, and fling,
At their return, up the high strand,
Begin, and cease, and then again begin,
With tremulous cadence slow, and bring
The <u>eternal</u> note of sadness in.

15 <u>Sophocles</u> long ago
Heard it on the <u>Aegean,</u> and it brought
Into his mind the turbid ebb and flow
Of human misery; <u>we</u>
Find <u>also</u> in the sound a thought,
20 Hearing it by this distant northern sea.

Symbol of romance

Contrast
Alliteration
Who is speaking, Male or Female,
To whom?

Visual image
Auditory image

Sound imitates sense

Time motif

Greek Tragedy
Literary and Historical allusions

Contrast: Dover & Aegean—
Sophocles and "we"

The Sea of Faith   Figure of Speech—Metaphor
Was once, too, at the full, and round earth's shore
Lay <u>like</u> the folds of a bright girdle furled.   Simile
<u>But now</u> I only hear   Contrast—Present & Past
25 Its melancholy, long, withdrawing roar,
Retreating, to the breath
of the <u>n</u>ight wind, down the vast edges drear   Change in mood of setting
And <u>n</u>aked shingles of the world.   Alliteration

Ah, <u>love,</u> let us be true   Tone
30 To one another! for the world, which <u>seems</u>   A key word
To lie before us <u>like</u> a land of dreams,   Simile
<u>So</u> various, <u>so</u> beautiful, <u>so</u> new,   Repetition
Hath really <u>n</u>either joy, <u>n</u>or love, <u>n</u>or light,
<u>N</u>or certitude, <u>n</u>or peace, <u>n</u>or help for pain;
35 And <u>we</u> are here as on a darkling plain   Change in context for "we"
Swept with confused alarms of struggle and flight,
Where ignorant armies clash by <u>night.</u>   Repeated from end of first line

Anonymous

Western Wind (English lyric)

Western wind, when wilt thou blow,
The small rain down can rain?
Christ, if my love were in my arms,
And I in my bed again!

Anonymous

Bonny Barbara Allan (traditional Scottish ballad)

It was in and about the Martinmas[1] time,
    even the green leaves were afalling,
That Sir John Graeme, in the West Country,
    Fell in love with Barbara Allan.

5 He sent his men down through the town,
    To the place where she was dwelling;
"O haste and come to my master dear,
    Gin[2] ye be Barbara Allan."

O hooly,[3] hooly rose she up,
10   To the place where he was lying,
And when she drew the curtain by:
    "Young man, I think you're dying."

"O it's I'm sick, and very, very sick,
    And 'tis a' for Barbara Allan."—
15 "O the better for me ye's never be,
    Tho your heart's blood were aspilling.

---

[1] Saint Martin's Day, November 11.
[2] If.
[3] Slowly.

1

"O dinna ye mind,[4] young man," said she,
    "When ye was in the tavern adrinking,
That ye made the health gae round and round,
20   And slighted Barbara Allan?"

He turned his face unto the wall,
    And death was with him dealing:
"Adieu, adieu, my dear friends all,
    And be kind to Barbara Allan."

25 And slowly, slowly raise she up,
    And slowly, slowly left him,
And sighing said she could not stay,
    Since death of life had reft him.

She had not gane a mile but twa,
30   When she heard the dead-bell ringing,
And every jow[5] that the dead-bell geid,
    It cried, "Woe to Barbara Allan!"

"O mother, mother, make my bed!
    O make it saft and narrow!
35 Since my love died for me today,
    I'll die for him tomorrow."

[4] Don't you remember.
[5] Stroke.

Anonymous

Sir Patrick Spence (traditional Scottish ballad)

The king sits in Dumferling toune,
    Drinking the blude-reid wine:
"O whar will I get guid sailor
    To sail this schip of mine?"

5 Up and spak an eldern knicht,
    Sat at the kings richt kne:
"Sir Patrick Spence is the best sailor
    That sails upon the se."

The king has written a braid letter,
10   And signed it wi' his hand,
And sent it to Sir Patrick Spence,
    Was walking on the sand.

The first line that Sir Patrick red,
    A loud lauch lauchèd he;
15 The next line that Sir Patrick red,
    The teir blinded his ee.

"O wha[1] is this has don this deid,
    This ill deid don to me,
To send me out this time o' the yeir,
20   To sail upon the se!

"Mak haste, mak haste, my mirry men all,
    Our guid schip sails the morne."
"O say na sae[2] my master deir,
    For I feir a deadlie storme.

25 "Late late yestreen I saw the new moone,
    Wi' the auld moone in hir arme,
And I feir, I feir, my deir master,
    That we will cum to harme."

[1] Who.
[2] Not so.

O our Scots nobles wer richt laith[3]
30   To weet[4] their cork-heild schoone;[5]
Bot lang owre[6] a' the play wer playd,
    Their hats they swam aboone.[7]

O lang, lang may their ladies sit,
    Wi' their fans into their hand,
35 Or ere they se Sir Patrick Spence
    Cum sailing to the land.

O lang, lang may the ladies stand,
    Wi' their gold kems[8] in their hair,
Waiting for their ain[9] deir lords,
40   For they'll se thame na mair.

Haf owre,[10] haf owre to Aberdour,
    It's fiftie fadom deip,
And their lies guid Sir Patrick Spence,
    Wi' the Scots lords at his feit.

Margaret Atwood, 1939–

You Fit into Me (1971)

you fit into me
like a hook into an eye

a fish hook
an open eye

---

[3] Loath.
[4] Wet.
[5] Shoes.
[6] Before.
[7] Above.
[8] Combs.
[9] Own.
[10] Halfway over.

W. H. Auden, 1907–1973

Musée des Beaux Arts (1940)

About suffering they were never wrong,
The Old Masters: how well they understood
Its human position; how it takes place
While someone else is eating or opening a window or just walking
    dully along
5 How, when the aged are reverently, passionately waiting
For the miraculous birth, there always must be
Children who did not specially want it to happen, skating
On a pond at the edge of the wood:
They never forgot
10 That even the dreadful martyrdom must run its course
Anyhow in a corner, some untidy spot
Where the dogs go on with their doggy life and the torturer's horse
Scratches its innocent behind on a tree.
In Brueghel's *Icarus,* for instance: how everything turns away
15 Quite leisurely from the disaster; the ploughman may
Have heard the splash, the forsaken cry,
But for him it was not an important failure; the sun shone
As it had to on the white legs disappearing into the green
Water; and the expensive delicate ship that must have seen
20 Something amazing, a boy falling out of the sky,
Had somewhere to get to and sailed calmly on.

Elizabeth Bishop, 1911–1979

The Fish (1946)

I caught a tremendous fish
and held him beside the boat
half out of water, with my hook
fast in a corner of his mouth.
5 He didn't fight.
He hadn't fought at all.
He hung a grunting weight,
battered and venerable
and homely. Here and there
10 his brown skin hung in strips
like ancient wallpaper,
and its pattern of darker brown
was like wallpaper:
shapes like full-blown roses
15 stained and lost through age.
He was speckled with barnacles,
fine rosettes of lime,
and infested
with tiny white sea-lice,
20 and underneath two or three
rags of green weed hung down.
While his gills were breathing in
the terrible oxygen
—the frightening gills,
25 fresh and crisp with blood,
that can cut so badly—
I thought of the coarse white flesh
packed in like feathers,
the big bones and the little bones,
30 the dramatic reds and blacks
of his shiny entrails,
and the pink swim-bladder
like a big peony.
I looked into his eyes
35 which were far larger than mine
but shallower, and yellowed,
the irises backed and packed
with tarnished tinfoil
seen through the lenses

40 of old scratched isinglass.
They shifted a little, but not
to return my stare.
—It was more like the tipping
of an object toward the light.
45 I admired his sullen face,
the mechanism of his jaw,
and then I saw
that from his lower lip
—if you could call it a lip—
50 grim, wet, and weaponlike,
hung five old pieces of fish-line,
or four and a wire leader
with the swivel still attached,
with all their five big hooks
55 grown firmly in his mouth.
A green line, frayed at the end
where he broke it, two heavier lines,
and a fine black thread
still crimped from the strain and snap
60 when it broke and he got away.
Like medals with their ribbons
frayed and wavering,
a five-haired beard of wisdom
trailing from his aching jaw.
65 I stared and stared
and victory filled up
the little rented boat,
from the pool of bilge
where oil had spread a rainbow
70 around the rusted engine
to the bailer rusted orange,
the sun-cracked thwarts,
the oarlocks on their strings,
the gunnels—until everything
75 was rainbow, rainbow, rainbow!
And I let the fish go.

William Blake, 1757–1827

The Tyger (1794)

Tyger! Tyger! burning bright
In the forests of the night,
What immortal hand or eye
Could frame thy fearful symmetry?

5 In what distant deeps or skies
Burnt the fire of thine eyes?
On what wings dare he aspire?
What the hand dare seize the fire?

And what shoulder, and what art,
10 Could twist the sinews of thy heart?
And when thy heart began to beat,
What dread hand? and what dread feet?

What the hammer? what the chain?
In what furnace was thy brain?
15 What the anvil? what dread grasp
Dare its deadly terrors clasp?

When the stars threw down their spears,
And watered heaven with their tears,
Did he smile his work to see?
20 Did he who made the Lamb make thee?

Tyger! Tyger! burning bright
In the forests of the night,
What immortal hand or eye
Dare frame thy fearful symmetry?

William Blake, 1757–1827

The Lamb (1789)

    Little Lamb, who made thee?
    Dost thou know who made thee?
Gave thee life & bid thee feed,
By the stream & o'er the mead;
5 Gave thee clothing of delight,
Softest clothing wooly bright;
Gave thee such a tender voice,
Making all the vales rejoice!
    Little Lamb, who made thee?
10   Dost thou know who made thee?

    Little Lamb, I'll tell thee,
    Little Lamb, I'll tell thee:
He is calléd by thy name,
For he calls himself a Lamb:
15 He is meek & he is mild,
He became a little child:
I a child & thou a lamb,
We are calléd by his name.
    Little Lamb, God bless thee!
20   Little Lamb, God bless thee!

William Blake, 1757–1827

The Sick Rose (1794)

O Rose, thou art sick.
The invisible worm
That flies in the night
In the howling storm

5 Has found out thy bed
Of crimson joy,
And his dark secret love
Does thy life destroy.

Anne Bradstreet, 1612?–1672

To My Dear and Loving Husband (1678)

If ever two were one, then surely we.
If ever man were lov'd by wife, then thee;
If ever wife was happy in a man,
Compare with me ye women if you can.
5 I prize thy love more than whole mines of gold,
Or all the riches that the East doth hold.
My love is such that rivers cannot quench,
Nor ought but love from thee, give recompence.
Thy love is such I can no way repay,
10 The heavens reward thee manifold I pray.
Then while we live, in love let's so persever,
That when we live no more, we may live ever.

Gwendolyn Brooks, 1917–

We Real Cool (1960)

The Pool Players.
Seven at the Golden Shovel.

We real cool. We
Left School. We

Lurk late. We
Strike straight. We
5 Sing sin. We
Thin gin. We

Jazz June. We
Die soon.

Gwendolyn Brooks, 1917–

The Bean Eaters (1960)

They eat beans mostly, this old yellow pair.
Dinner is a casual affair.
Plain chipware on a plain and creaking wood,
Tin flatware.

5   Two who are Mostly Good.
Two who have lived their day,
But keep on putting on their clothes
And putting things away.

And remembering . . .
10   Remembering, with twinklings and twinges,
As they lean over the beans in their rented back room that is full of
    beads and receipts and dolls and clothes, tobacco crumbs, vases
    and fringes.

Elizabeth Barrett Browning, 1806–1861

How Do I Love Thee? (1850)

How do I love thee? Let me count the ways.
I love thee to the depth and breadth and height
My soul can reach, when feeling out of sight
For the ends of being and ideal grace.
5   I love thee to the level of every day's
Most quiet need, by sun and candle-light.
I love thee freely, as men strive for right.
I love thee purely, as they turn from praise.
I love thee with the passion put to use
10   In my old griefs, and with my childhood's faith.
I love thee with a love I seemed to lose
With my lost saints. I love thee with the breath,
Smiles, tears, of all my life; and, if God choose,
I shall but love thee better after death.

Robert Browning, 1812–1889

My Last Duchess (1842)

FERRARA

That's my last Duchess painted on the wall,
Looking as if she were alive. I call
That piece a wonder, now: Frà Pandolf's[1] hands
Worked busily a day, and there she stands.
5 Will't please you sit and look at her? I said
"Frà Pandolf" by design, for never read
Strangers like you that pictured countenance,
The depth and passion of its earnest glance,
But to myself they turned (since none puts by
10 The curtain I have drawn for you, but I)
And seemed as they would ask me, if they durst,
How such a glance came there; so, not the first
Are you to turn and ask thus. Sir, 'twas not
Her husband's presence only, called that spot
15 Of joy into the Duchess' cheek: perhaps
Frà Pandolf chanced to say "Her mantle laps
Over my lady's wrist too much," or "Paint
Must never hope to reproduce the faint
Half-flush that dies along her throat": such stuff
20 Was courtesy, she thought, and cause enough
For calling up that spot of joy. She had
A heart—how shall I say?—too soon made glad,
Too easily impressed; she liked whate'er
She looked on, and her looks went everywhere.
25 Sir, 'twas all one! My favor at her breast,
The dropping of the daylight in the West,
The bough of cherries some officious fool
Broke in the orchard for her, the white mule
She rode with round the terrace—all and each
30 Would draw from her alike the approving speech,
Or blush, at least. She thanked men—good! but thanked
Somehow—I know not how—as if she ranked

---

[1] "Brother" Pandolf, a fictive painter.

My gift of a nine-hundred-years-old name
With anybody's gift. Who'd stoop to blame
35 This sort of trifling? Even had you skill
In speech—(which I have not)—to make your will
Quite clear to such an one, and say, "Just this
Or that in you disgusts me; here you miss,
Or there exceed the mark"—and if she let
40 Herself be lessoned so, nor plainly set
Her wits to yours, forsooth, and made excuse
—E'en then would be some stooping; and I choose
Never to stoop. Oh sir, she smiled, no doubt,
Whene'er I passed her; but who passed without
45 Much the same smile? This grew; I gave commands;
Then all smiles stopped together. There she stands
As if alive. Will't please you rise? We'll meet
The company below, then. I repeat,
The Count your master's known munificence
50 Is ample warrant that no just pretense
Of mine for dowry will be disallowed;
Though his fair daughter's self, as I avowed
At starting, is my object. Nay, we'll go
Together down, sir. Notice Neptune,[2] though,
55 Taming a sea horse, thought a rarity,
Which Claus of Innsbruck[3] cast in bronze for me!

[2] God of the sea.
[3] An imaginary—or unidentified—sculptor. The Count of Tyrol's capital was at Innsbruck, Austria.

Robert Burns, 1759–1796

Oh, My Love Is Like a Red, Red Rose (1796)

Oh, my love is like a red, red rose
    That's newly sprung in June;
My love is like the melody
    That's sweetly played in tune.

5 So fair art thou, my bonny lass,
    So deep in love am I;
And I will love thee still, my dear,
    Till a' the seas gang[1] dry.

Till a' the seas gang dry, my dear,
10   And the rocks melt wi' the sun;
And I will love thee still, my dear,
    While the sands o' life shall run.

And fare thee weel, my only love!
    And fare thee weel awhile!
15 And I will come again, my love
    Though it were ten thousand mile.

[1] Go.

George Gordon, Lord Byron, 1788–1824

She Walks in Beauty (1814)

From Hebrew Melodies

I
She walks in Beauty, like the night
   Of cloudless climes and starry skies;
And all that's best of dark and bright
   Meet in her aspect and her eyes:
5 Thus mellowed to that tender light
   Which Heaven to gaudy day denies.

II
One shade the more, one ray the less,
   Had half impaired the nameless grace
Which waves in every raven tress,
10   Or softly lightens o'er her face;
Where thoughts serenely sweet express,
   How pure, how dear their dwelling-place.

III
And on that cheek, and o'er that brow,
   So soft, so calm, yet eloquent,
15 The smiles that win, the tints that glow,
   But tell of days in goodness spent,
A mind at peace with all below,
   A heart whose love is innocent!

Thomas Campion, 1567–1620

There Is a Garden in Her Face (1617)

There is a garden in her face
Where roses and white lilies grow;
   A heav'nly paradise is that place
Wherein all pleasant fruits do flow.
5   There cherries grow which none may buy
   Till "Cherry-ripe" themselves do cry.

Those cherries fairly do enclose
Of orient pearl a double row,
   Which when her lovely laughter shows,
10 They look like rose-buds filled with snow;
   Yet them nor peer nor prince can buy,
   Till "Cherry-ripe" themselves do cry.

Her eyes like angels watch them still;
Her brows like bended bows do stand,
15   Threat'ning with piercing frowns to kill
All that attempt, with eye or hand
   Those sacred cherries to come nigh
   Till "Cherry-ripe" themselves do cry.

Lewis Carroll, 1832–1898

Jabberwocky (1871)

'Twas brillig, and the slithy toves
   Did gyre and gimble in the wabe:
All mimsy were the borogoves,
   And the mome raths outgrabe.

5 "Beware the Jabberwock, my son!
   The jaws that bite, the claws that catch!
Beware the Jubjub bird, and shun
   The frumious Bandersnatch!"

He took his vorpal sword in hand;
10   Long time the manxome foe he sought—
So rested he by the Tumtum tree
   And stood awhile in thought.

And, as in uffish thought he stood,
   The Jabberwock, with eyes of flame,
15 Came whiffling through the tulgey wood,
   And burbled as it came!

One, two! One, two! And through and through
   The vorpal blade went snicker-snack!
He left it dead, and with its head
20   He went galumphing back.

"And hast thou slain the Jabberwock?
   Come to my arms, my beamish boy!
O frabjous day! Callooh, Callay!"
   He chortled in his joy.

25 'Twas brillig, and the slithy toves
   Did gyre and gimble in the wabe:
All mimsy were the borogoves,
   And the mome raths outgrabe.

Lucille Clifton, 1936—

homage to my hips (1987)

these hips are big hips
they need space to
move around in.
they don't fit into little
5 petty places. these hips
are free hips.
they don't like to be held back.
these hips have never been enslaved.
they go where they want to go.
10 they do what they want to do.
these hips are mighty hips.
these hips are magic hips.
i have known them
to put a spell on a man and
15 spin him like a top!

Samuel Taylor Coleridge, 1772–1834

Kubla Khan[1] (1797–1798)

Or, a Vision in a Dream. A Fragment.

In Xanadu did Kubla Khan
A stately pleasure-dome decree:
Where Alph,[2] the sacred river, ran
Through caverns measureless to man
5   Down to a sunless sea.
So twice five miles of fertile ground
With walls and towers were girdled round;
And there were gardens bright with sinuous rills,
Where blossomed many an incense-bearing tree;
10 And here were forests ancient as the hills,
Enfolding sunny spots of greenery.

But oh! that deep romantic chasm which slanted
Down the green hill athwart a cedarn cover!
A savage place! as holy and enchanted
15 As e'er beneath a waning moon was haunted
By woman wailing for her demon-lover!
And from this chasm, with ceaseless turmoil seething,
As if this earth in fast thick pants were breathing,
A mighty fountain momently was forced:
20 Amid whose swift half-intermitted burst
Huge fragments vaulted like rebounding hail,
Or chaffy grain beneath the thresher's flail:
And 'mid these dancing rocks at once and ever
It flung up momently the sacred river.
25 Five miles meandering with a mazy motion
Through wood and dale the sacred river ran,
Then reached the caverns measureless to man,
And sank in tumult to a lifeless ocean:
And 'mid this tumult Kubla heard from far

---

[1] Coleridge mythologizes the actual Kublai Khan, founder of a thirteenth-century Mongol empire, as well as the Chinese city of Xanadu.
[2] Probably derived from the Greek river Alpheus, whose waters, according to legend, rose from the Ionian Sea in Sicily as the fountain of Arethusa.

30 Ancestral voices prophesying war!
　　The shadow of the dome of pleasure
　　Floated midway on the waves;
　　Where was heard the mingled measure
　　From the fountain and the caves.
35 It was a miracle of rare device,
　　A sunny pleasure-dome with caves of ice!

　　A damsel with a dulcimer
　　In a vision once I saw:
　　It was an Abyssinian maid,
40　　And on her dulcimer she played,
　　Singing of Mount Abora.[3]
　　Could I revive within me
　　Her symphony and song,
　　To such a deep delight 'twould win me,
45 That with music loud and long,
　　I would build that dome in air,
　　That sunny dome! those caves of ice!
　　And all who heard should see them there,
　　And all should cry, Beware! Beware!
50 His flashing eyes, his floating hair!
　　Weave a circle round him thrice,[4]
　　And close your eyes with holy dread,
　　For he on honey-dew hath fed,
　　And drunk the milk of Paradise.

[3] Some scholars see a reminiscence here of John Milton's *Paradise Lost* IV, 280–82: "where Abassin kings their issue guard / Mount Amara, though this by some supposed / True Paradise under the Ethiop Line."
[4] A magic ritual, to keep away intruding spirits.

Hart Crane, 1899–1932

Proem: To Brooklyn Bridge (1930)

How many dawns, chill from his rippling rest
The seagull's wings shall dip and pivot him,
Shedding white rings of tumult, building high
Over the chained bay waters Liberty—

5 Then, with inviolate curve, forsake our eyes
As apparitional as sails that cross
Some page of figures to be filed away;
—Till elevators drop us from our day . . .

I think of cinemas, panoramic sleights
10 With multitudes bent toward some flashing scene
Never disclosed, but hastened to again,
Foretold to other eyes on the same screen;

And Thee, across the harbor, silver-paced
As though the sun took step of thee, yet left
15 Some motion ever unspent in thy stride,—
Implicitly thy freedom staying thee!

Out of some subway scuttle, cell or loft
A bedlamite[1] speeds to thy parapets,
Tilting there momently, shrill shirt ballooning,
20 A jest falls from the speechless caravan.

Down Wall, from girder into street noon leaks,
A rip-tooth of the sky's acetylene;
All afternoon the cloud-flown derricks turn . . .
Thy cables breathe the North Atlantic still.

25 And obscure as that heaven of the Jews,
Thy guerdon[2] . . . Accolade thou dost bestow
Of anonymity time cannot raise:
Vibrant reprieve and pardon thou dost show.

---

[1] bedlamite: insane person, here bent on suicide.
[2] guerdon: reward; accolade: ceremony or salute of praise or approval.

O harp and altar, of the fury fused,
30 (How could mere toil align thy choiring strings!)
Terrific threshold of the prophet's pledge,
Prayer of pariah, and the lover's cry,—

Again the traffic lights that skim thy swift
Unfractioned idiom, immaculate sigh of stars,
35 Beading thy path—condense eternity:
And we have seen night lifted in thine arms.

Under thy shadow by the piers I waited;
Only in darkness is thy shadow clear.
The City's fiery parcels all undone,
40 Already snow submerges an iron year . . .

O Sleepless as the river under thee,
Vaulting the sea, the prairies' dreaming sod,
Unto us lowliest sometime sweep, descend
And of the curveship lend a myth to God.

Countee Cullen, 1903–1946

For a Lady I Know (1925)

She even thinks that up in heaven
   Her class lies late and snores,
While poor black cherubs rise at seven
   To do celestial chores.

e. e. cummings, 1894–1962

in Just—[1] (1923)

in Just—
spring   when the world is mud—
luscious the little
lame balloonman
5 whistles   far   and wee

and eddieandbill come
running from marbles and
piracies and it's
spring

10 when the world is puddle-wonderful
the queer
old balloonman whistles
far   and   wee
and bettyandisbel come dancing

15 from hop-scotch and jump-rope and

it's
spring
and
      the

20   goat-footed

balloonMan   whistles
far
and
wee

[1] Also known as "Chansons Innocentes I."

e. e. cummings, 1894–1962

Buffalo Bill's (1923)

Buffalo Bill's
defunct
     who used to
     ride a watersmooth-silver
5   stallion
and break onetwothreefourfive pigeonsjustlikethat
                          Jesus

he was a handsome man
            and what i want to know is
10 how do you like your blueeyed boy
Mister Death

Emily Dickinson, 1830–1886

Because I Could Not Stop for Death (1863)

Because I could not stop for Death—
He kindly stopped for me—
The Carriage held but just Ourselves—
And Immortality.

5 We slowly drove—He knew no haste
And I had put away
My labor and my leisure too,
For His Civility—

We passed the School, where Children strove
10 At Recess—in the Ring—
We passed the Fields of Gazing Grain—
We passed the Setting Sun—

Or rather—He passed Us—
The Dews drew quivering and chill—
15 For only Gossamer, my Gown—
My Tippet[1]—only Tulle—

We paused before a House that seemed
A Swelling of the Ground—
The Roof was scarcely visible—
20 The Cornice—in the Ground—

Since then—'tis Centuries—and yet
Feels shorter than the Day
I first surmised the Horses' Heads
Were toward Eternity—

Emily Dickinson, 1830–1886

I Heard a Fly Buzz—When I Died (c. 1862)

I heard a Fly buzz—when I died—
The Stillness in the Room
Was like the Stillness in the Air—
Between the Heaves of Storm—

5 The Eyes around—had wrung them dry—
And Breaths were gathering firm
For that last Onset—when the King
Be witnessed—in the Room—

I willed my Keepsakes—Signed away
10 What portion of me be
Assignable—and then it was
There interposed a Fly—

With Blue—uncertain stumbling Buzz—
Between the light—and me—
15 And then the Windows failed—and then
I could not see to see—

[1] Cape.

Emily Dickinson, 1830–1886

I Taste a Liquor Never Brewed (1861)

I taste a liquor never brewed—
From Tankards scooped in Pearl—
Not all the Frankfort Berries[1]
Yield such an Alcohol!

5 Inebriate of Air—am I—
And Debauchee of Dew—
Reeling—thro endless summer days—
From inns of Molten Blue—

When "Landlords" turn the drunken Bee
10 Out of the Foxglove's door—
When Butterflies—renounce their "drams"—
I shall but drink the more!

Till Seraphs swing their snowy Hats—
And Saints—to windows run—
15 To see the little Tippler
From Manzanilla[2] come!

---

[1] This line is a variant reading for the usually accepted "Not all the Vats upon the Rhine." In both cases, the poet refers to German wine.
[2] A pale Spanish sherry.

Emily Dickinson, 1830–1886

I Like to See It Lap the Miles (1891)

I like to see it lap the Miles—
And lick the Valleys up—
And stop to feed itself at Tanks—
And then—prodigious step

5 Around a Pile of Mountains—
And supercilious peer
In Shanties—by the sides of Roads—
And then a Quarry pare

To fit its Ribs
10 And crawl between
Complaining all the while
In horrid—hooting stanza—
Then chase itself down Hill—

And neigh like Boanerges[1]—
15 Then—punctual as a Star
Stop—docile and omnipotent
At its own stable door—

---

[1] A vociferous preacher and orator. Also, the name, meaning "son of thunder," Jesus gave to apostles John and James because of their fiery zeal.

John Donne, 1572–1631

Song (1633)

Go and catch a falling star,
   Get with child a mandrake root,[1]
Tell me where all past years are,
   Or who cleft the Devil's foot,

5 Teach me to hear mermaids singing,
   Or to keep off envy's stinging,
      And find
      What wind
Serves to advance an honest mind.

10 If thou be'st borne to strange sights,
   Things invisible to see,
Ride ten thousand days and nights,
   Till age snow white hairs on thee,
Thou, when thou return'st, wilt tell me
15   All strange wonders that befell thee,
      And swear
      Nowhere
Lives a woman true, and fair.

If thou findst one, let me know,
20   Such a pilgrimage were sweet—
Yet do not, I would not go,
   Though at next door we might meet;
Though she were true, when you met her,
   And last, till you write your letter,
25   Yet she
      Will be
False, ere I come, to two, or three.

---

[1] The mandrake root (or mandragora), which is forked and resembles the lower part of the human body, was thought to be an aphrodisiac.

John Donne, 1572–1631

Batter My Heart,
Three-Personed God (c. 1610)

Batter my heart, three-personed God, for You
As yet but knock, breathe, shine, and seek to mend.
That I may rise and stand, o'erthrow me, and bend
Your force to break, blow, burn, and make me new.
5 I, like an usurped town to another due,
Labor to admit You, but Oh! to no end.
Reason, Your viceroy in me, me should defend,
But is captived, and proves weak or untrue.
Yet dearly I love You, and would be lovèd fain,
10 But am betrothed unto Your enemy;
Divorce me, untie or break that knot again;
Take me to You, imprison me, for I,
Except You enthrall me, never shall be free,
Nor ever chaste, except You ravish me.

John Donne, 1572–1631

Death Be Not Proud (c. 1610)

Death be not proud, though some have callèd thee
Mighty and dreadful, for thou art not so;
For those whom thou think'st thou dost overthrow
Die not, poor death, nor yet canst thou kill me.
5 From rest and sleep, which but thy pictures be,
Much pleasure, then from thee much more must flow,
And soonest our best men with thee do go,
Rest of their bones, and soul's delivery.
Thou art slave to fate, chance, kings, and desperate men,
10 And dost with poison, war, and sickness dwell,
And poppy, or charms can make us sleep as well,
And better than thy stroke; why swell'st thou then?
One short sleep past, we wake eternally,
And death shall be no more; death, thou shalt die.

Rita Dove, 1952–

Daystar (1986)

She wanted a little room for thinking:
but she saw diapers steaming on the line,
a doll slumped behind the door.
So she lugged a chair behind the garage
5 to sit out the children's naps.

Sometimes there were things to watch—
the pinched armor of a vanished cricket,
a floating maple leaf. Other days
she stared until she was assured
10 when she closed her eyes
she'd see only her own vivid blood.

She had an hour, at best, before Liza appeared
pouting from the top of the stairs.
And just *what* was mother doing
15 out back with the field mice? Why,

building a palace. Later
that night when Thomas rolled over and
lurched into her, she would open her eyes
and think of the place that was hers
20 for an hour—where
she was nothing,
pure nothing, in the middle of the day.

Michael Drayton, 1563–1631

Since There's No Help (1619)

Since there's no help, come let us kiss and part;
Nay, I have done, you get no more of me,
And I am glad, yea, glad with all my heart
That thus so cleanly I myself can free;
5 Shake hands for ever, cancel all our vows,
And when we meet at any time again,
Be it not seen in either of our brows
That we one jot of former love retain.
Now at the last gasp of Love's latest breath,
10 When, his pulse failing, Passion speechless lies,
When Faith is kneeling by his bed of death,
And Innocence is closing up his eyes,
   Now if thou wouldst, when all have given him over,
   From death to life thou mightst him yet recover.

T. S. Eliot, 1888–1965

Journey of the Magi[1] (1927)

"A cold coming we had of it,
Just the worst time of the year
For a journey, and such a long journey:
The ways deep and the weather sharp,
5 The very dead of winter"[2]
And the camels galled, sore-footed, refractory,
Lying down in the melting snow.
There were times we regretted
The summer palaces on slopes, the terraces,
10 And the silken girls bringing sherbet.
Then the camel men cursing and grumbling
And running away, and wanting their liquor and women,
And the night-fires going out, and the lack of shelters,
And the cities hostile and the towns unfriendly
15 And the villages dirty and charging high prices:
A hard time we had of it.
At the end we preferred to travel all night,
Sleeping in snatches,
With the voices singing in our ears, saying
20 That this was all folly.

Then at dawn we came down to a temperate valley,
Wet, below the snow line, smelling of vegetation;
With a running stream and a water-mill beating the darkness,
And three trees[3] on the low sky,
25 And an old white horse[4] galloped away in the meadow.
Then we came to a tavern with vine-leaves over the lintel,
Six hands at an open door dicing for pieces of silver,[5]
And feet kicking the empty wine-skins.
But there was no information, and so we continued
30 And arrived at evening, not a moment too soon
Finding the place; it was (you may say) satisfactory.

---

[1] In the poem, one of the three wise men who ventured east to pay tribute to the infant Jesus (see Matthew 12:1–12) recalls the experience.
[2] The five quoted lines are adapted from a passage in a 1622 Christmas Day sermon by Bishop Lancelot Andrewes.
[3] Refers to the three crosses at Calvary (see Luke 23:32–33).
[4] Refers to the white horse of the conquering Christ in Revelation 19:11–16.
[5] Echoes the soldiers dicing for Christ's garments, as well as his betrayal by Judas.

All this was a long time ago, I remember,
And I would do it again, but set down
This set down
35 This: were we led all that way for
Birth or Death? There was a Birth, certainly,
We had evidence and no doubt. I had seen birth and death,
But had thought they were different; this Birth was
Hard and bitter agony for us, like Death, our death.
40 We returned to our places, these Kingdoms,
But no longer at ease here, in the old dispensation,
With an alien people clutching their gods.
I should be glad of another death.

T. S. Eliot, 1888–1965

The Love Song of J. Alfred Prufrock (1917)

S'io credesse che mia risposta fosse
A persona che mai tornasse al mondo,
Questa fiamma staria senza più scosse.
Ma perciocche giammai di questo fondo
Non tornò vivo alcun, s'i'odo il vero,
Senza tema d'infamia ti rispondo.[1]

Let us go then, you and I,
When the evening is spread out against the sky
Like a patient etherized upon a table;
Let us go, through certain half-deserted streets,
5 The muttering retreats
Of restless nights in one-night cheap hotels
And sawdust restaurants with oyster-shells:
Streets that follow like a tedious argument
Of insidious intent

---

[1] The epigraph is from Dante's *Inferno*, Canto XXVII. In response to the poet's question about his identity, Guido da Montefelto, who for his sin of fraud must spend eternity wrapped in flames, replies: "If I thought that I was speaking to someone who could go back to the world, this flame would shake me no more. But since from this place nobody ever returns alive, if what I hear is true, I answer you without fear of infamy."

10 To lead you to an overwhelming question . . .
Oh, do not ask, "What is it?"
Let us go and make our visit.

In the room the women come and go
Talking of Michelangelo.

15 The yellow fog that rubs its back upon the window-panes,
The yellow smoke that rubs its muzzle on the window-panes
Licked its tongue into the corners of the evening,
Lingered upon the pools that stand in drains,
Let fall upon its back the soot that falls from chimneys,
20 Slipped by the terrace, made a sudden leap,
And seeing that it was a soft October night,
Curled once about the house, and fell asleep.

And indeed there will be time
For the yellow smoke that slides along the street,
25 Rubbing its back upon the window-panes;
There will be time, there will be time
To prepare a face to meet the faces that you meet;
There will be time to murder and create,
And time for all the works and days[2] of hands
30 That lift and drop a question on your plate;
Time for you and time for me,
And time yet for a hundred indecisions,
And for a hundred visions and revisions,
Before the taking of a toast and tea.

35 In the room the women come and go
Talking of Michelangelo.

And indeed there will be time
To wonder, "Do I dare?" and, "Do I dare?"
Time to turn back and descend the stair,
40 With a bald spot in the middle of my hair—
(They will say: "How his hair is growing thin!")
My morning coat, my collar mounting firmly to the chin,
My necktie rich and modest, but asserted by a simple pin—
(They will say: "But how his arms and legs are thin!")
45 Do I dare
Disturb the universe?
In a minute there is time
For decisions and revisions which a minute will reverse.

---

[2] *Works and Days* is the title of a work by the eighth-century B.C. Greek Hesiod, whose poem celebrates farmwork.

For I have known them all already, known them all—
50 Have known the evenings, mornings, afternoons,
I have measured out my life with coffee spoons;
I know the voices dying with a dying fall[3]
Beneath the music from a farther room.
　　So how should I presume?

55 And I have known the eyes already, known them all—
The eyes that fix you in a formulated phrase,
And when I am formulated, sprawling on a pin,
When I am pinned and wriggling on the wall,
Then how should I begin
60 To spit out all the butt-ends of my days and ways?
　　And how should I presume?

And I have known the arms already, known them all—
Arms that are braceleted and white and bare
(But in the lamplight, downed with light brown hair!)
65 Is it perfume from a dress
That makes me so digress?
Arms that lie along a table, or wrap about a shawl.
　　And should I then presume?
　　And how should I begin?

◆　◆　◆

70 Shall I say, I have gone at dusk through narrow streets
And watched the smoke that rises from the pipes
Of lonely men in shirt-sleeves, leaning out of windows? . . .

I should have been a pair of ragged claws
Scuttling across the floors of silent seas.

◆　◆　◆

75 And the afternoon, the evening, sleeps so peacefully!
Smoothed by long fingers,
Asleep . . . tired . . . or it malingers,
Stretched on the floor, here beside you and me.
Should I, after tea and cakes and ices,
80 Have the strength to force the moment to its crisis?
But though I have wept and fasted, wept and prayed,

---

[3] Allusion to Orsino's speech in *Twelfth Night* (I, i), "That strain again! It hath a dying fall."

Though I have seen my head (grown slightly bald) brought in upon a
    platter,[4]
I am no prophet—and here's no great matter;
I have seen the moment of my greatness flicker,
85 And I have seen the eternal Footman[5] hold my coat, and snicker,
And in short, I was afraid.

And would it have been worth it, after all,
After the cups, the marmalade, the tea,
Among the porcelain, among some talk of you and me,
90 Would it have been worth while,
To have bitten off the matter with a smile,
To have squeezed the universe into a ball
To roll it toward some overwhelming question,
To say: "I am Lazarus,[6] come from the dead,
95 Come back to tell you all, I shall tell you all"—
If one, settling a pillow by her head,
    Should say: "That is not what I meant at all.
    That is not it, at all."

And would it have been worth it, after all,
100 Would it have been worth while,
After the sunsets and the dooryards and the sprinkled streets,
After the novels, after the teacups, after the skirts that trail along the
    floor—
And this, and so much more?—
It is impossible to say just what I mean!
105 But as if a magic lantern threw the nerves in patterns on a screen:
Would it have been worth while
If one, settling a pillow or throwing off a shawl,
And turning toward the window, should say:
    "That is not it at all,
110   That is not what I meant, at all."

◆ ◆ ◆

No! I am not Prince Hamlet, nor was meant to be;
Am an attendant lord, one that will do

---

[4] Like John the Baptist, who was beheaded by King Herod (see Matthew 14:3-11).
[5] Perhaps death, or fate.
[6] Lazarus was raised from the dead by Christ (see John 11:1-44).

To swell a progress,[7] start a scene or two,
Advise the prince; no doubt, an easy tool,
115 Deferential, glad to be of use,
Politic, cautious, and meticulous;
Full of high sentence,[8] but a bit obtuse;
At times, indeed, almost ridiculous—
Almost, at times, the Fool.

120 I grow old . . . I grow old . . .
I shall wear the bottoms of my trousers rolled.

Shall I part my hair behind? Do I dare to eat a peach?
I shall wear white flannel trousers, and walk upon the beach.
I have heard the mermaids singing, each to each.

125 I do not think that they will sing to me.

I have seen them riding seaward on the waves
Combing the white hair of the waves blown back
When the wind blows the water white and black.

We have lingered in the chambers of the sea
130 By sea-girls wreathed with seaweed red and brown
Till human voices wake us, and we drown.

Carolyn Forché, 1950–

The Colonel (1978)

What you have heard is true. I was in his house. His wife carried a tray of
coffee and sugar. His daughter filed her nails, his son went out for the night.
There were daily papers, pet dogs, a pistol on the cushion beside him. The
moon swung bare on its black cord over the house. On the television was a
cop show. It was in English. Broken bottles were embedded in the walls
around the house to scoop the kneecaps from a man's legs or cut his hands
to lace. On the windows there were gratings like those in liquor stores. We
had dinner, rack of lamb, good wine, a gold bell was on the table for calling
the maid. The maid brought green mangoes, salt, a type of bread. I was asked

---

[7] Here, in the Elizabethan sense of a royal journey.
[8] Opinions.

how I enjoyed the country. There was a brief commercial in Spanish. His wife took everything away. There was some talk then of how difficult it had become to govern. The parrot said hello on the terrace. The colonel told it to shutup, and pushed himself from the table. My friend said to me with his eyes: say nothing. The colonel returned with a sack used to bring groceries home. He spilled many human ears on the table. They were like dried peach halves. There is no other way to say this: He took one of them in his hands, shook it in our faces, dropped it into a water glass. It came alive there. I am tired of fooling around he said. As for the rights of anyone, tell your people they can go fuck themselves. He swept the ears to the floor with his arm and held the last of his wine in the air. Something for your poetry, no? he said. Some of the ears on the floor caught this scrap of his voice. Some of the ears on the floor were pressed to the ground.

Robert Frost, 1874–1963

The Road Not Taken (1915)

Two roads diverged in a yellow wood,
And sorry I could not travel both
And be one traveler, long I stood
And looked down one as far as I could
5 To where it bent in the undergrowth;

Then took the other, as just as fair,
And having perhaps the better claim,
Because it was grassy and wanted wear;
Though as for that the passing there
10 Had worn them really about the same,

And both that morning equally lay
In leaves no step had trodden black.
Oh, I kept the first for another day!
Yet knowing how way leads on to way,
15 I doubted if I should ever come back.

I shall be telling this with a sigh
Somewhere ages and ages hence:
Two roads diverged in a wood, and I—
I took the one less traveled by,
20 And that has made all the difference.

Robert Frost, 1874–1963

Stopping by Woods on a Snowy Evening (1923)

Whose woods these are I think I know.
His house is in the village though;
He will not see me stopping here
To watch his woods fill up with snow.

5 My little horse must think it queer
To stop without a farmhouse near
Between the woods and frozen lake
The darkest evening of the year.

He gives his harness bells a shake
10 To ask if there is some mistake.
The only other sound's the sweep
Of easy wind and downy flake.

The woods are lovely, dark and deep,
But I have promises to keep,
15 And miles to go before I sleep,
And miles to go before I sleep.

Robert Frost, 1874–1963

Mending Wall (1914)

Something there is that doesn't love a wall,
That sends the frozen-ground-swell under it,
And spills the upper boulders in the sun;
And makes gaps even two can pass abreast.
5 The work of hunters is another thing:
I have come after them and made repair
Where they have left not one stone on a stone,
But they would have the rabbit out of hiding,
To please the yelping dogs. The gaps I mean,

10 No one has seen them made or heard them made,
But at spring mending-time we find them there.
I let my neighbor know beyond the hill;
And on a day we meet to walk the line
And set the wall between us once again.
15 We keep the wall between us as we go.
To each the boulders that have fallen to each.
And some are loaves and some so nearly balls
We have to use a spell to make them balance:
"Stay where you are until our backs are turned!"
20 We wear our fingers rough with handling them.
Oh, just another kind of outdoor game,
One on a side. It comes to little more:
There where it is we do not need the wall:
He is all pine and I am apple orchard.
25 My apple trees will never get across
And eat the cones under his pines, I tell him.
He only says, "Good fences make good neighbors."
Spring is the mischief in me, and I wonder
If I could put a notion in his head:
30 "*Why* do they make good neighbors? Isn't it
Where there are cows? But here there are no cows.
Before I built a wall I'd ask to know
What I was walling in or walling out,
And to whom I was like to give offense.
35 Something there is that doesn't love a wall,
That wants it down." I could say "Elves" to him,
But it's not elves exactly, and I'd rather
He said it for himself. I see him there
Bringing a stone grasped firmly by the top
40 In each hand, like an old-stone savage armed.
He moves in darkness as it seems to me,
Not of woods only and the shade of trees.
He will not go behind his father's saying,
And he likes having thought of it so well
45 He says again, "Good fences make good neighbors."

Robert Frost, 1874–1963

Acquainted with the Night (1928)

I have been one acquainted with the night.
I have walked out in rain—and back in rain.
I have outwalked the furthest city light.

I have looked down the saddest city lane.
5 I have passed by the watchman on his beat
And dropped my eyes, unwilling to explain.

I have stood still and stopped the sound of feet
When far away an interrupted cry
Came over houses from another street,

10 But not to call me back or say good-by;
And further still at an unearthly height,
One luminary clock against the sky

Proclaimed the time was neither wrong nor right.
I have been one acquainted with the night.

Tess Gallagher, 1932–

Sudden Journey (1984)

Maybe I'm seven in the open field—
the straw-grass so high
only the top of my head makes a curve
of brown in the yellow. Rain then.
5 First a little. A few drops on my
wrist, the right wrist. More rain.
My shoulders, my chin. Until I'm looking up
to let my eyes take the bliss.
I open my face. Let the teeth show. I
10 pull my shirt down past the collar-bones.
I'm still a boy under my breast spots.
I can drink anywhere. The rain. My
skin shattering. Up suddenly, needing
to gulp, turning with my tongue, my arms out
15 running, running in the hard, cold plenitude
of all those who reach earth by falling.

Nikki Giovanni, 1943–

Nikki-Rosa (1968)

childhood remembrances are always a drag
if you're Black
you always remember things like living in Woodlawn[1]
with no inside toilet
5 and if you become famous or something
they never talk about how happy you were to have your mother
all to yourself and
how good the water felt when you got your bath from one of those
big tubs that folk in chicago barbecue in

---

[1] A predominantly black suburb of Cincinnati, Ohio.

10 and somehow when you talk about home
it never gets across how much you
understood their feelings
as the whole family attended meetings about Hollydale
and even though you remember
15 your biographers never understand
your father's pain as he sells his stock
and another dream goes
and though you're poor it isn't poverty that
concerns you
20 and though they fought a lot
it isn't your father's drinking that makes any difference
but only that everybody is together and you
and your sister have happy birthdays and very good christmasses
and I really hope no white person ever has cause to write about me
25 because they never understand Black love is Black wealth and they'll
probably talk about my hard childhood and never understand that
all the while I was quite happy

Allen Ginsberg, 1926–

A Supermarket in California (1956)

What thoughts I have of you tonight, Walt Whitman,[1] for I walked
down the sidestreets under the trees with a headache self-conscious
looking at the full moon.

In my hungry fatigue, and shopping for images, I went into the
5 neon fruit supermarket, dreaming of your enumerations!

What peaches and what penumbras! Whole families shopping at
night! Aisles full of husbands! Wives in the avocados, babies in the
tomatoes!—and you, Garcia Lorca,[2] what were you doing down by the
watermelons?

---

[1] Walt Whitman (1819-1892)—American poet. Whitman's poems frequently praise the commonplace and often contain lengthy "enumerations."
[2] Federico García Lorca (1899-1936)—Spanish poet and dramatist.

10   I saw you, Walt Whitman, childless, lonely old grubber, poking
among the meats in the refrigerator and eyeing the grocery boys.[3]

I heard you asking questions of each: Who killed the pork chops?
What price bananas? Are you my Angel?

I wandered in and out of the brilliant stacks of cans following you,
15   and followed in my imagination by the store detective.

We strode down the open corridors together in our solitary fancy
tasting artichokes, possessing every frozen delicacy, and never passing the cashier.

Where are we going, Walt Whitman? The doors close in an hour.
20   Which way does your beard point tonight?

(I touch your book[4] and dream of our odyssey in the supermarket
and feel absurd.)

Will we walk all night through solitary streets? The trees add shade
to shade, lights out in the houses, we'll both be lonely.

25   Will we stroll dreaming of the lost America of love past blue auto-
mobiles in driveways, home to our silent cottage?

Ah, dear father, graybeard, lonely old courage-teacher, what America did you have when Charon[5] quit poling his ferry and you got out
on a smoking bank and stood watching the boat disappear on the
30   black waters of Lethe?[6]

Thomas Hardy, 1840–1928

Channel Firing (1914)

That night your great guns, unawares,
Shook all our coffins[1] as we lay,
And broke the chancel window-squares,
We thought it was the Judgment Day

---

[3] Whitman's sexual orientation is the subject of much debate. Ginsberg is suggesting here that Whitman was homosexual.

[4] *Leaves of Grass.*

[5] In Greek mythology, the ferryman who transported the souls of the dead across the Styx and Acheron rivers to the underworld.

[6] The mythological underworld river whose waters caused the dead to forget their former lives.

[1] For centuries, it has been the practice in England to bury people under the flooring or in the basements of churches.

5   And sat upright. While drearisome
    Arose the howl of wakened hounds:
    The mouse let fall the altar-crumb,
    The worms drew back into the mounds,

    The glebe[2] cow drooled. Till God called, "No;
10 It's gunnery practice out at sea
    Just as before you went below;
    The world is as it used to be:

    "All nations striving strong to make
    Red war yet redder. Mad as hatters
15 They do no more for Christés sake
    Than you who are helpless in such matters.

    "That this is not the judgment hour
    For some of them's a blessed thing,
    For if it were they'd have to scour
20 Hell's floor for so much threatening. . . .

    "Ha, ha. It will be warmer when
    I blow the trumpet (if indeed
    I ever do; for you are men,
    And rest eternal sorely need)."

25 So down we lay again. "I wonder,
    Will the world ever saner be,"
    Said one, "than when He sent us under
    In our indifferent century!"

    And many a skeleton shook his head.
30 "Instead of preaching forty year,"
    My neighbor Parson Thirdly said,
    "I wish I had stuck to pipes and beer."

    Again the guns disturbed the hour,
    Roaring their readiness to avenge,
35 As far inland as Stourton Tower.[3]
    And Camelot,[4] and starlit Stonehenge.[5]

---

[2] A small field.
[3] Erected in the eighteenth century in Wiltshire, England, to commemorate King Alfred the Great's defeat of the Danes in 878.
[4] Legendary site of King Arthur's court.
[5] A group of stones on Salisbury Plain, believed by many, including Hardy, to be the site of ancient druidic rituals.

Thomas Hardy, 1840–1928

The Convergence of the Twain (1914)

LINES ON THE LOSS OF THE "TITANIC"[1]

I

In a solitude of the sea
Deep from human vanity,
And the Pride of Life that planned her, stilly couches she.

II

Steel chambers, late the pyres
5 Of her salamandrine[2] fires,
Cold currents thrid,[3] and turn to rhythmic tidal lyres.

III

Over the mirrors meant
To glass the opulent
The sea-worm crawls—grotesque, slimed, dumb, indifferent.

IV

10 Jewels in joy designed
To ravish the sensuous mind
Lie lightless, all their sparkles bleared and black and blind.

V

Dim moon-eyed fishes near
Gaze at the gilded gear
15 And query: "What does this vaingloriousness down here?" . . .

VI

Well: while was fashioning
This creature of cleaving wing,
The Immanent Will that stirs and urges everything

VII

Prepared a sinister mate
20 For her—so gaily great—
A Shape of Ice, for the time far and dissociate.

---

[1] On the night of April 14, 1912, the *Titanic,* the largest ship afloat and on her maiden voyage to New York from Southampton, collided with an iceberg in the North Atlantic and sank in less than three hours; 1,500 of 2,206 passengers were lost.
[2] Bright red; the salamander was supposed to be able to live in fire.
[3] Thread.

VIII
 And as the smart ship grew
 In stature, grace, and hue,
In shadowy silent distance grew the Iceberg too.

IX
25 Alien they seemed to be;
 No mortal eye could see
The intimate welding of their later history,

X
 Or sign that they were bent
 By paths coincident
On being anon twin halves of one august event,

XI
 Till the Spinner of the Years
 Said "Now!" And each one hears,
And consummation comes, and jars two hemispheres.

Robert Hayden, 1913–1980

Those Winter Sundays (1962)

Sundays too my father got up early
and put his clothes on in the blueblack cold,
then with cracked hands that ached
from labor in the weekday weather made
5 banked fires blaze. No one ever thanked him.

I'd wake and hear the cold splintering, breaking.
When the rooms were warm, he'd call,
and slowly I would rise and dress,
fearing the chronic angers of that house,

10 Speaking indifferently to him,
who had driven out the cold
and polished my good shoes as well.
What did I know, what did I know
of love's austere and lonely offices?

Seamus Heaney, 1939—

Digging (1966)

Between my finger and my thumb
The squat pen rests; snug as a gun.

Under my window, a clean rasping sound
When the spade sinks into gravelly ground:
5 My father, digging. I look down

Till his straining rump among the flowerbeds
Bends low, comes up twenty years away
Stooping in rhythm through potato drills
Where he was digging.

10 The coarse boot nestled on the lug, the shaft
Against the inside knee was levered firmly.
He rooted out tall tops, buried the bright edge deep
To scatter new potatoes that we picked
Loving their cool hardness in our hands.

15 By God, the old man could handle a spade.
Just like his old man.

My grandfather cut more turf in a day
Than any other man on Toner's bog.
Once I carried him milk in a bottle
20 Corked sloppily with paper. He straightened up
To drink it, then fell to right away

Nicking and slicing neatly, heaving sods
Over his shoulder, going down and down
For the good turf. Digging.

25 The cold smell of potato mould, the squelch and slap
Of soggy peat, the curt cuts of an edge
Through living roots awaken in my head.
But I've no spade to follow men like them.

Between my finger and my thumb
30 The squat pen rests.
I'll dig with it.

George Herbert, 1593–1633

Easter Wings (1633)

Lord, who createdst man in wealth and store,
Though foolishly he lost the same,
Decaying more and more
Till he became
Most poor;
    With thee
    Oh, let me rise
As larks, harmoniously,
And sing this day thy victories;
Then shall the fall further the flight in me.

My tender age in sorrow did begin:
And still with sicknesses and shame
Thou didst so punish sin,
That I became
Most thin.
    With thee
    Let me combine,
And feel this day thy victory;
For, if I imp my wing on thine,
Affliction shall advance the flight in me.

Robert Herrick, 1591–1674

Delight in Disorder (1648)

A sweet disorder in the dress
Kindles in clothes a wantonness.
A lawn[1] about the shoulders thrown
Into a fine distractión;
5 An erring lace, which here and there
Enthralls the crimson stomacher;[2]
A cuff neglectful, and thereby
Ribbons to flow confusedly;
A winning wave, deserving note,
10 In the tempestuous petticoat;
A careless shoestring, in whose tie
I see a wild civility;
Do more bewitch me than when art
Is too precise in every part.

[1] A shawl made of fine fabric.
[2] A decorative covering for the breasts.

Robert Herrick, 1591–1674

To the Virgins, to Make Much of Time (1646)

Gather ye rosebuds while ye may,
    Old Time is still a-flying;
And this same flower that smiles today,
    Tomorrow will be dying.

5 The glorious lamp of heaven, the sun,
    The higher he's a-getting,
The sooner will his race be run,
    And nearer he's to setting.

That age is best which is the first,
10   When youth and blood are warmer;
But being spent, the worse, and worst
    Times still succeed the former.

Then be not coy, but use your time,
    And while ye may, go marry;
15 For having lost but once your prime,
    You may forever tarry.

Gerard Manley Hopkins, 1844–1889

God's Grandeur (1877)

The world is charged with the grandeur of God.
   It will flame out, like shining from shook foil;
   It gathers to a greatness, like the ooze of oil
Crushed. Why do men then now not reck his rod?
5 Generations have trod, have trod, have trod;
   And all is seared with trade; bleared, smeared with toil;
   And wears man's smudge and shares man's smell: the soil
Is bare now, nor can foot feel, being shod.
And for all this, nature is never spent;
10   There lives the dearest freshness deep down things;
And though the last lights off the black West went
   Oh, morning, at the brown brink eastward, springs—
Because the Holy Ghost over the bent
   World broods with warm breast and with ah! bright wings.

Gerard Manley Hopkins, 1844–1889

Pied Beauty (1877)

Glory be to God for dappled things—
   For skies of couple-color as a brinded[1] cow;
     For rose-moles all in stipple upon trout that swim;
Fresh-firecoal chestnut-falls; finches' wings;
5   Landscape plotted and pieced—fold, fallow, and plow;
     And áll trádes, their gear and tackle and trim.[2]

All things counter, original, spare, strange;
   Whatever is fickle, freckled (who knows how?)
     With swift, slow; sweet, sour; adazzle, dim;
10 He fathers-forth whose beauty is past change:
        Praise him.

---

[1] Brindled (streaked).
[2] Equipment.

A. E. Housman, 1859–1936

To an Athlete Dying Young (1896)

The time you won your town the race
We chaired you through the market-place;
Man and boy stood cheering by,
And home we brought you shoulder-high.

5 Today, the road all runners come,
Shoulder-high we bring you home,
And set you at your threshold down,
Townsman of a stiller town.

Smart lad, to slip betimes away
10 From fields where glory does not stay,
And early though the laurel grows
It withers quicker than the rose.

Eyes the shady night has shut
Cannot see the record cut,
15 And silence sounds no worse than cheers
After earth has stopped the ears.

Now you will not swell the rout
Of lads that wore their honors out,
Runners whom renown outran
20 And the name died before the man.

So set, before its echoes fade,
The fleet foot on the sill of shade,
And hold to the low lintel up
The still-defended challenge-cup.

25 And round that early-laureled head
Will flock to gaze the strengthless dead,
And find unwithered on its curls
The garland briefer than a girl's.

Langston Hughes, 1902–1967

Dream Deferred (1951)

What happens to a dream deferred?

Does it dry up
like a raisin in the sun?

Or fester like a sore—
5   And then run?
Does it stink like rotten meat?
Or crust and sugar over—
like a syrupy sweet?

Maybe it just sags
10   like a heavy load.

Or does it explode?

Langston Hughes, 1902–1967

Negro (1926)

I am a Negro:
    Black as the night is black,
    Black like the depths of my Africa.

I've been a slave:
5   Caesar told me to keep his door-steps clean.
    I brushed the boots of Washington.

I've been a worker:
    Under my hand the pyramids arose.
    I made mortar for the Woolworth Building.

10 I've been a singer:
    All the way from Africa to Georgia
    I carried my sorrow songs.
    I made ragtime.

I've been a victim:
15   The Belgians cut off my hands in the Congo.
    They lynch me still in Mississippi.

I am a Negro:
    Black as the night is black,
    Black like the depths of my Africa.

Randall Jarrell, 1914–1965

The Death of the Ball Turret Gunner (1945)

From my mother's sleep I fell into the State
And I hunched in its belly till my wet fur froze.
Six miles from earth, loosed from its dream of life,
I woke to black flak and the nightmare fighters.
5 When I died they washed me out of the turret with a hose.

Ben Jonson, 1573?–1637

On My First Son (1603)

Farewell, thou child of my right hand,[1] and joy.
My sin was too much hope of thee, loved boy;
Seven years thou wert lent to me, and I thee pay,
Exacted by thy fate, on the just day.[2]
5 Oh, could I lose all father now. For why
Will man lament the state he should envỳ?—
To have so soon 'scaped world's and flesh's rage,
And, if no other misery, yet age.
Rest in soft peace, and asked, say, "Here doth lie
10 Ben Jonson his best piece of poetry,"
For whose sake henceforth all his vows be such
As what he loves may never like[3] too much.

[1] Translation of the Hebrew name of Benjamin, Jonson's son.
[2] The very day.
[3] Thrive.

Ben Jonson, 1573?–1637

To Celia (1616)

Drink to me only with thine eyes,
    And I will pledge with mine;
Or leave a kiss but in the cup,
    And I'll not ask for wine.
5 The thirst that from the soul doth rise
    Doth ask a drink divine;
But might I of Jove's nectar sup,
    I would not change for thine.

Donald Justice, 1925–

On the Death of Friends in Childhood (1960)

We shall not ever meet them bearded in heaven,
Nor sunning themselves among the bald of hell;
If anywhere, in the deserted schoolyard at twilight,
Forming a ring, perhaps, or joining hands
5 In games whose very names we have forgotten.
Come, memory, let us seek them there in the shadows.

John Keats, 1795–1821

Ode on a Grecian Urn[1] (1819, 1820)

1

Thou still unravish'd bride of quietness,
    Thou foster-child of silence and slow time,
Sylvan[2] historian, who canst thus express
A flowery tale more sweetly than our rhyme:
5 What leaf-fring'd legend haunts about thy shape
    Of deities or mortals, or of both,
        In Tempe[3] or the dales of Arcady?[4]
    What men or gods are these? What maidens loth?
What mad pursuit? What struggle to escape?
10   What pipes and timbrels? What wild ecstasy?

2

Heard melodies are sweet, but those unheard
    Are sweeter; therefore, ye soft pipes, play on;
Not to the sensual ear, but, more endear'd,
    Pipe to the spirit ditties of no tone:
15 Fair youth, beneath the trees, thou canst not leave
    Thy song, nor ever can those trees be bare;
        Bold lover, never, never canst thou kiss,
Though winning near the goal—yet, do not grieve;
        She cannot fade, though thou hast not thy bliss,
20   For ever wilt thou love, and she be fair!

---

[1] Though many urns similar to the one Keats describes actually exist, the subject of the poem is purely imaginary.
[2] Pertaining to woods or forests.
[3] A beautiful valley in Greece.
[4] The valleys of Arcadia, a mountainous region on the Greek peninsula. Like Tempe, they represent a rustic pastoral ideal.

3

Ah, happy, happy boughs! that cannot shed
    Your leaves, nor ever bid the spring adieu;
And, happy melodist, unwearied,
    For ever piping songs for ever new;
25 More happy love! more happy, happy love!
    For ever warm and still to be enjoy'd,
      For ever panting, and for ever young;
All breathing human passion far above,
    That leaves a heart high-sorrowful and cloy'd,
30   A burning forehead, and a parching tongue.

4

Who are these coming to the sacrifice?
    To what green altar, O mysterious priest,
Lead'st thou that heifer lowing at the skies,
    And all her silken flanks with garlands drest?
35 What little town by river or sea shore,
    Or mountain-built with peaceful citadel,
      Is emptied of this folk, this pious morn?
And, little town, thy streets for evermore
    Will silent be; and not a soul to tell
40   Why thou art desolate, can e'er return.

5

O Attic[5] shape! Fair attitude! with brede[6]
    Of marble men and maidens overwrought,[7]
With forest branches and the trodden weed;
    Thou, silent form, dost tease us out of thought
45 As doth eternity: Cold Pastoral!
    When old age shall this generation waste,
      Thou shalt remain, in midst of other woe
Than ours, a friend to man, to whom thou say'st,
    "Beauty is truth, truth beauty,"—that is all
50   Ye know on earth, and all ye need to know.

[5] Characteristic of Athens or Athenians.
[6] Braid.
[7] Elaborately ornamented.

John Keats, 1775–1821

Ode to a Nightingale (1819)

1

My heart aches, and a drowsy numbness pains
  My sense, as though of hemlock I had drunk,
Or emptied some dull opiate to the drains
  One minute past, and Lethe-wards[1] had sunk:
5 'Tis not through envy of thy happy lot,
  But being too happy in thine happiness,—
    That thou, light-winged Dryad[2] of the trees,
    In some melodious plot
Of beechen green, and shadows numberless,
10   Singest of summer in full-throated ease.

2

O, for a draught of vintage! that hath been
  Cool'd a long age in the deep-delved earth,
Tasting of Flora[3] and the country green,
  Dance, and Provençal song,[4] and sunburnt mirth!
15 O for a beaker full of the warm South,
  Full of the true, the blushful Hippocrene,[5]
    With beaded bubbles winking at the brim,
    And purple-stained mouth;
That I might drink, and leave the world unseen,
20   And with thee fade away into the forest dim:

[1] Toward Lethe, the river in Hades whose waters cause forgetfulness.
[2] In Greek mythology, a tree spirit, a wood nymph.
[3] Roman goddess of flowers; also, the flowers themselves.
[4] Provence, in southern France, was famous in medieval times for its troubadors, who wrote and performed love songs.
[5] Fountain of the Muses on Mt. Helicon; a source of poetic inspiration.

3

Fade far away, dissolve, and quite forget
    What thou among the leaves hast never known,
The weariness, the fever, and the fret
    Here, where men sit and hear each other groan;
25 Where palsy shakes a few, sad, last gray hairs,
    Where youth grows pale, and spectre-thin, and dies;
        Where but to think is to be full of sorrow
           And leaden-eyed despairs,
    Where Beauty cannot keep her lustrous eyes,
30   Or new Love pine at them beyond to-morrow.

4

Away! away! for I will fly to thee,
    Not charioted by Bacchus[6] and his pards,
But on the viewless wings of Poesy,
    Though the dull brain perplexes and retards:
35 Already with thee! tender is the night,
    And haply the Queen-Moon is on her throne,
        Cluster'd around by all her starry Fays,[7]
           But here there is no light,
    Save what from heaven is with the breezes blown
40   Through verdurous glooms and winding mossy ways.

5

I cannot see what flowers are at my feet,
    Nor what soft incense hangs upon the boughs,
But, in embalmed[8] darkness, guess each sweet
    Wherewith the seasonable month endows
45 The grass, the thicket, and the fruit-tree wild;
    White hawthorn, and the pastoral eglantine,[9]
        Fast fading violets cover'd up in leaves;
           And mid-May's eldest child,
    The coming musk-rose, full of dewy wine,
50   The murmurous haunt of flies on summer eves.

[6] Greek god of wine.
[7] Fairies.
[8] Perfumed.
[9] Sweetbrier, or honeysuckle.

6

Darkling[10] I listen; and, for many a time
　　I have been half in love with easeful Death,
Call'd him soft names in many a mused[11] rhyme,
　　To take into the air my quiet breath;
55　Now more than ever seems it rich to die,
　　To cease upon the midnight with no pain,
　　　　While thou art pouring forth thy soul abroad
　　　　　In such an ecstasy!
　　Still wouldst thou sing, and I have ears in vain—
60　　　To thy high requiem become a sod.

7

Thou wast not born for death, immortal Bird!
　　No hungry generations tread thee down;
The voice I hear this passing night was heard
　　In ancient days by emperor and clown:
65　Perhaps the self-same song that found a path
　　Through the sad heart of Ruth,[12] when, sick for home,
　　　　She stood in tears amid the alien corn,[13]
　　　　　The same that oft-times hath
　　Charm'd magic casements, opening on the foam
70　　　Of perilous seas, in faery lands forlorn.

8

Forlorn! the very word is like a bell
　　To toll me back from thee to my sole self!
Adieu! the fancy[14] cannot cheat so well
　　As she is fam'd to do, deceiving elf.
75　Adieu! adieu! thy plaintive anthem[15] fades
　　Past the near meadows, over the still stream,
　　　　Up the hill-side; and now 'tis buried deep
　　　　　In the next valley-glades:
　　Was it a vision, or a waking dream?
80　　　Fled is that music:—Do I wake or sleep?

---

[10] In the dark.
[11] Meditated.
[12] The widow of Mahlon in the biblical Book of Ruth. She is sad and homesick because she left her home with her mother-in-law to go to Bethlehem. While there she married Boaz, a rich landowner. She was the great-grandmother of King David.
[13] Wheat.
[14] Imagination. Compare "the viewless wings of Poesy," line 33.
[15] Hymn.

John Keats, 1795–1821

On First Looking into Chapman's Homer[1] (1816)

Much have I traveled in the realms of gold,
   And many goodly states and kingdoms seen;
   Round many western islands have I been
Which bards in fealty to Apollo[2] hold.
5 Oft of one wide expanse had I been told
   That deep-browed Homer ruled as his demesne,[3]
   Yet did I never breathe its pure serene[4]
Till I heard Chapman speak out loud and bold.
Then felt I like some watcher of the skies
10   When a new planet swims into his ken;
Or like stout Cortez[5] when with eagle eyes
   He stared at the Pacific—and all his men
Looked at each other with a wild surmise—
   Silent, upon a peak in Darien.[6]

---

[1] The translation of Homer by Elizabethan poet George Chapman.
[2] Greek god of light, truth, reason, male beauty; associated with music and poetry.
[3] Realm, domain.
[4] Air, atmosphere.
[5] It was Vasco de Balboa (not Hernando Cortez as Keats suggests) who first saw the Pacific Ocean, from "a peak in Darien," in Panama.
[6] Former name of the Isthmus of Panama.

John Keats, 1795–1821

To Autumn (1819)

I

Season of mists and mellow fruitfulness,
    Close bosom-friend of the maturing sun;
Conspiring with him how to load and bless
    With fruit the vines that round the thatch-eves run;
5 To bend with apples the mossed cottage-trees,
    And fill all fruit with ripeness to the core;
        To swell the gourd, and plump the hazel shells
With a sweet kernel; to set budding more,
    And still more, later flowers for the bees,
10   Until they think warm days will never cease,
        For Summer has o'er-brimmed their clammy cells.

II

Who hath not seen thee oft amid thy store?
    Sometimes whoever seeks abroad may find
Thee sitting careless on a granary floor,
15   Thy hair soft-lifted by the winnowing wind,[1]
Or on a half-reaped furrow sound asleep,
    Drowsed with the fume of poppies, while thy hook[2]
        Spares the next swath and all its twinéd flowers:
And sometimes like a gleaner thou dost keep
20   Steady thy laden head across a brook;
    Or by a cider-press, with patient look,
        Thou watchest the last oozings hours by hours.

[1] Which sifts the grain from the chaff.
[2] Scythe or sickle.

III

Where are the songs of Spring? Ay, where are they?
    Think not of them, thou hast thy music too—
25 While barréd clouds bloom the soft-dying day,
    And touch the stubble-plains with rosy hue;
Then in a wailful choir the small gnats mourn
      Among the river sallows,[3] borne aloft
        Or sinking as the light wind lives or dies;
30 And full-grown lambs loud bleat from hilly bourn,[4]
      Hedge-crickets sing; and now with treble soft
    The red-breast whistles from a garden-croft,[5]
      And gathering swallows twitter in the skies.

Galway Kinnell, 1927–

Blackberry Eating (1980)

I love to go out in late September
among the fat, overripe, icy, black blackberries
to eat blackberries for breakfast,
the stalks very prickly, a penalty
5 they earn for knowing the black art
of blackberry-making; and as I stand among them
lifting the stalks to my mouth, the ripest berries
fall almost unbidden to my tongue,
as words sometimes do, certain peculiar words
10 like *strengths* or *squinched,*
many-lettered, one-syllabled lumps,
which I squeeze, squinch open, and splurge well
in the silent, startled, icy, black language
of blackberry-eating in late September.

[3] Willows.
[4] Domain.
[5] An enclosed garden near a house.

Maxine Kumin, 1925–

Woodchucks (1972)

Gassing the woodchucks didn't turn out right.
The knockout bomb from the Feed and Grain Exchange
was featured as merciful, quick at the bone
and the case we had against them was airtight,
5   both exits shoehorned shut with puddingstone,[1]
but they had a sub-sub-basement out of range.

Next morning they turned up again, no worse
for the cyanide than we for our cigarettes
and state-store Scotch, all of us up to scratch.
10 They brought down the marigolds as a matter of course
and then took over the vegetable patch
nipping the broccoli shoots, beheading the carrots.

The food from our mouths, I said, righteously thrilling
to the feel of the .22, the bullets' neat noses.
15 I, a lapsed pacifist fallen from grace
puffed with Darwinian pieties for killing,
now drew a bead on the littlest woodchuck's face.
He died down in the everbearing roses.

Ten minutes later I dropped the mother. She
20 flipflopped in the air and fell, her needle teeth
still hooked in a leaf of early Swiss chard.
Another baby next. O one-two-three
the murderer inside me rose up hard,
the hawkeye killer came on stage forthwith.

25 There's one chuck left. Old wily fellow, he keeps
me cocked and ready day after day after day.
All night I hunt his humped-up form. I dream
I sight along the barrel in my sleep.
If only they'd all consented to die unseen
gassed underground the quiet Nazi way.

---

[1] A mixture of cement, pebbles, and gravel.

Denise Levertov 1923–

What Were They Like? (1966)

1) Did the people of Viet Nam
   use lanterns of stone?
2) Did they hold ceremonies
   to reverence the opening of buds?
3) Were they inclined to rippling laughter?
4) Did they use bone and ivory,
   jade and silver, for ornament?
5) Had they an epic poem?
6) Did they distinguish between speech and singing?

1) Sir, their light hearts turned to stone.
   It is not remembered whether in gardens
   stone lanterns illumined pleasant ways.
2) Perhaps they gathered once to delight in blossom,
   but after the children were killed
   there were no more buds.
3) Sir, laughter is bitter to the burned mouth.
4) A dream ago, perhaps. Ornament is for joy.
   All the bones were charred.
5) It is not remembered. Remember,
   most were peasants; their life
   was in rice and bamboo.
   When peaceful clouds were reflected in the paddies
   and the water buffalo stepped surely along terraces,
   maybe fathers told their sons old tales.
   When bombs smashed the mirrors
   there was time only to scream.
6) There is an echo yet, it is said,
   of their speech which was like a song.
   It is reported their singing resembled
   the flight of moths in moonlight.
   Who can say? It is silent now.

Robert Lowell, 1917–1977

Skunk Hour (1959)

For Elizabeth Bishop

Nautilus Island's hermit
heiress still lives through winter in her Spartan cottage;
her sheep still gaze above the sea.
Her son's a bishop. Her farmer
5 is first selectman[1] in our village;
she's in her dotage.

Thirsting for
the hierarchic privacy
of Queen Victoria's century,
10 she buys up all
the eyesores facing her shore,
and lets them fall.

The season's ill—
we've lost our summer millionaire,
15 who seemed to leap from an L. L. Bean[2]
catalogue. His nine-knot yawl
was auctioned off to lobstermen.
A red fox stain covers Blue Hill.

And now our fairy
20 decorator brightens his shop for fall;
his fishnet's filled with orange cork,
orange, his cobbler's bench and awl;
there is no money in his work,
he'd rather marry.

25 One dark night,
my Tudor Ford climbed the hill's skull;
I watched for love-cars. Lights turned down,
they lay together, hull to hull,
where the graveyard shelves on the town. . . .
30 My mind's not right.

---

[1] An elected New England town official.
[2] Famous old Maine sporting goods firm.

A car radio bleats,
"Love, O careless Love. . . . "[3] I hear
my ill-spirit sob in each blood cell,
as if my hand were at its throat. . . .
35 I myself am hell;
nobody's here—

only skunks, that search
in the moonlight for a bite to eat.
They march on their soles up Main Street:
40 white stripes, moonstruck eyes' red fire
under the chalk-dry and spar spire
of the Trinitarian Church.

I stand on top
of our back steps and breathe the rich air—
45 a mother skunk with her column of kittens swills the garbage pail.
She jabs her wedge head in a cup
of sour cream, drops her ostrich tail,
and will not scare.

[3] A popular song.

Archibald Macleish, 1892–1982

Ars Poetica[1] (1926)

A poem should be palpable and mute
As a globed fruit,

Dumb
As old medallions to the thumb,

5 Silent as the sleeve-worn stone
Of casement ledges where the moss has grown—

A poem should be wordless
As the flight of birds.

A poem should be motionless in time
10 As the moon climbs.

Leaving, as the moon releases
Twig by twig the night-entangled trees,

Leaving, as the moon behind the winter leaves,
Memory by memory the mind—

15 A poem should be motionless in time
As the moon climbs.

A poem should be equal to:
Not true.

For all the history of grief
20 An empty doorway and a maple leaf.

For love
The leaning grasses and two lights above the sea—

A poem should not mean
But be.

[1]"The Art of Poetry," title of a poetical treatise by the Roman poet Horace (65–8 B.C.).

Christopher Marlowe, 1564–1593

The Passionate Shepherd to His Love (1600)

Come live with me and be my love,
And we will all the pleasures prove
That valleys, groves, hills, and fields,
Woods, or steepy mountain yields.

5 And we will sit upon the rocks,
Seeing the shepherds feed their flocks
By shallow rivers, to whose falls
Melodious birds sing madrigals.

And I will make thee beds of roses
10 And a thousand fragrant posies,
A cap of flowers and a kirtle[1]
Embroidered all with leaves of myrtle;

A gown made of the finest wool
Which from our pretty lambs we pull;
15 Fair-linèd slippers for the cold,
With buckles of the purest gold;

A belt of straw and ivy buds,
With coral clasps and amber studs.
And if these pleasures may thee move,
20 Come live with me and be my love.

The shepherds' swains shall dance and sing
For thy delight each May morning.
If these delights thy mind may move,
Then live with me and be my love.

[1]Skirt.

Andrew Marvell, 1621–1678

To His Coy Mistress (1681)

Had we but world enough and time,
This coyness, lady, were no crime.
We would sit down and think which way
To walk, and pass our long love's day.
5 Thou by the Indian Ganges' side
Should'st rubies find; I by the tide
Of Humber[1] would complain. I would
Love you ten years before the Flood,
And you should, if you please, refuse
10 Till the conversion of the Jews.
My vegetable love should grow
Vaster than empires, and more slow.
An hundred years should go to praise
Thine eyes, and on thy forehead gaze,
15 Two hundred to adore each breast,
But thirty thousand to the rest.
An age at least to every part,
And the last age should show your heart.
For, lady, you deserve this state,
20 Nor would I love at lower rate.
　　But at my back I always hear
Time's wingèd chariot hurrying near,
And yonder all before us lie
Deserts of vast eternity.
25 Thy beauty shall no more be found,
Nor in thy marble vault shall sound
My echoing song; then worms shall try
That long preserved virginity,
And your quaint honor turn to dust,
30 And into ashes all my lust.
The grave's a fine and private place,
But none, I think, do there embrace.
　　Now therefore, while the youthful hue
Sits on thy skin like morning glew[2]
35 And while thy willing soul transpires

---

[1] An estuary in the east coast of England.
[2] Dew.

At every pore with instant fires,
Now let us sport us while we may;
And now, like amorous birds of prey,
Rather at once our time devour
40 Than languish in his slow-chapped[3] power.
Let us roll all our strength and all
Our sweetness up into one ball
And tear our pleasures with rough strife
Through the iron gates of life.
45 Thus, though we cannot make our sun
Stand still, yet we will make him run.

Edna St. Vincent Millay, 1892–1950

What Lips My Lips Have Kissed (1923)

What lips my lips have kissed, and where, and why,
I have forgotten, and what arms have lain
Under my head till morning; but the rain
Is full of ghosts tonight, that tap and sigh
5 Upon the glass and listen for reply,
And in my heart there stirs a quiet pain
For unremembered lads that not again
Will turn to me at midnight with a cry.
Thus in the winter stands the lonely tree,
10 Nor knows what birds have vanished one by one,
Yet knows its boughs more silent than before:
I cannot say what loves have come and gone,
I only know that summer sang in me
A little while, that in me sings no more.

---

[3] Slowly crushing.

John Milton, 1608–1674

When I Consider How My Light Is Spent[1] (1655?)

When I consider how my light is spent,
   Ere half my days in this dark world and wide,
   And that one talent[2] which is death to hide
Lodged with me useless, though my soul more bent
5 To serve therewith my Maker, and present
   My true account, lest He returning chide;
   "Doth God exact day-labor, light denied?"
I fondly[3] ask. But Patience, to prevent
That murmur, soon replies, "God doth not need
10   Either man's work or His own gifts. Who best
   Bear His mild yoke, they serve Him best. His state
Is kingly: thousands at His bidding speed,
   And post o'er land and ocean without rest;
   They also serve who only stand and wait."

Marianne Moore, 1887–1972

Poetry (1921)

I too, dislike it: there are things that are important beyond all this
   fiddle.
   Reading it, however, with a perfect contempt for it, one discovers
     in it
after all, a place for the genuine.
   Hands that can grasp, eyes
5   that can dilate, hair that can rise
     if it must, these things are important not because a

---

[1] A meditation on his blindness.
[2] See Jesus' parable of the talents in Matthew 25:14–30.
[3] Foolishly.

high-sounding interpretation can be put upon them but because they are
   useful. When they become so derivative as to become unintelligible,
   the same thing may be said for all of us, that we
10   do not admire what
   we cannot understand: the bat
      holding on upside down or in quest of something to

eat, elephants pushing, a wild horse taking a roll, a tireless wolf under
   a tree, the immovable critic twitching his skin like a horse that
      feels a
15   flea, the base-
ball fan, the statistician—
      nor is it valid
         to discriminate against "business documents and

school-books";[1] all these phenomena are important. One must make a
20   distinction
   however: when dragged into prominence by half poets, the result is
      not poetry,
   nor till the poets among us can be
      "literalists of
25   the imagination"[2]—above
      insolence and triviality and can present

for inspection, "imaginary gardens with real toads in them," shall
      we have
   it. In the meantime, if you demand on the one hand,
   the raw material of poetry in
30   all its rawness and
   that which is on the other hand
      genuine, you are interested in poetry.

[1] Moore quotes the *Diaries of Tolstoy* (New York, 1917): "Where the boundary between prose and poetry lies, I shall never be able to understand. . . . Poetry is verse; prose is verse. Or else poetry is everything with the exception of business documents and books."
[2] A reference (given by Moore) to W. B. Yeats's "William Blake and His Illustration (in *Ideas of Good and Evil,* 1903): "The limitation of his view was from the very intensity of his vision; he was a too literal realist of the imagination as others are of nature because he believed that the figures seen by the mind's eye, when exhalted by inspiration were 'external existences,' symbols of divine essences, he hated every grace of style that might obscure their liniments."

Howard Nemerov, 1920–1991

Life Cycle of Common Man (1960)

Roughly figured, this man of moderate habits,
This average consumer of the middle class,
Consumed in the course of his average life span
Just under half a million cigarettes,
5 Four thousand fifths of gin and about
A quarter as much vermouth; he drank
Maybe a hundred thousand cups of coffee,
And counting his parents' share it cost
Something like half a million dollars
10 To put him through life. How many beasts
Died to provide him with meat, belt and shoes
Cannot be certainly be said.
                              But anyhow,
It is in this way that a man travels through time,
Leaving behind him a lengthening trail
15 Of empty bottles and bones, of broken shoes,
Frayed collars and worn out or outgrown
Diapers and dinnerjackets, silk ties and slickers.

Given the energy and security thus achieved,
He did . . . ? What? The usual things, of course,
20 The eating, dreaming, drinking and begetting,
And he worked for the money which was to pay
For the eating, et cetera, which were necessary
If he were to go on working for the money, et cetera,
But chiefly he talked. As the bottles and bones
25 Accumulated behind him, the words proceeded
Steadily from the front of his face as he
Advanced into the silence and made it verbal.
Who can tally the tale of his words? A lifetime
Would barely suffice for their repetition;
30 If you merely printed all his commas the result
Would be a very large volume, and the number of times
He said "thank you" or "very little sugar, please,"
Would stagger the imagination. There were also
Witticisms, platitudes, and statements beginning
35 "It seems to me" or "As I always say."
Consider the courage in all that, and behold the man

Walking into deep silence, with the ectoplastic
Cartoon's balloon of speech proceeding
Steadily out of the front of his face, the words
40 Borne along on the breath which is his spirit
Telling the numberless tale of his untold Word
Which makes the world his apple, and forces him to eat.

Sharon Olds, 1942–

The One Girl at the Boys Party (1983)

When I take my girl to the swimming party
I set her down among the boys. They tower and
bristle, she stands there smooth and sleek,
her math scores unfolding in the air around her.
5 They will strip to their suits, her body hard and
indivisible as a prime number,
they'll plunge in the deep end, she'll subtract
her height from ten feet, divide it into
hundreds of gallons of water, the numbers
10 bouncing in her mind like molecules of chlorine
in the bright blue pool. When they climb out,
her ponytail will hang its pencil lead
down her back, her narrow silk suit
with hamburgers and french fries printed on it
15 will glisten in the brilliant air, and they will
see her sweet face, solemn and
sealed, a factor of one, and she will
see their eyes, two each,
their legs, two each, and the curves of their sexes,
20 one each, and in her head she'll be doing her
wild multiplying, as the drops
sparkle and fall to the power of a thousand from her body.

Sharon Olds, 1942–

Sex Without Love (1984)

How do they do it, the ones who make love
without love? Beautiful as dancers,
gliding over each other like ice-skaters
over the ice, fingers hooked
5 inside each other's bodies, faces
red as steak, wine, wet as the
children at birth whose mothers are going to
give them away. How do they come to the
come to the   come to the   God   come to the
10 still waters, and not love
the one who came there with them, light
rising slowly as steam off their joined
skin? These are the true religious,
the purists, the pros, the ones who will not
15 accept a false Messiah, love the
priest instead of the God. They do not
mistake the lover for their own pleasure,
they are like great runners: they know they are alone
with the road surface, the cold, the wind,
20 the fit of their shoes, their over-all cardio-
vascular health—just factors, like the partner
in the bed, and not the truth, which is the
single body alone in the universe
against its own best time.

Sharon Olds, 1942–

The Victims (1984)

    When Mother divorced you, we were glad. She took it and
    took it, in silence, all those years and then
    kicked you out, suddenly, and her
    kids loved it. Then you were fired, and we
5 grinned inside, the way people grinned when
    Nixon's helicopter lifted off the South
    Lawn for the last time.[1] We were tickled
    to think of your office taken away,
    your secretaries taken away,
10 your lunches with three double bourbons,
    your pencils, your reams of paper. Would they take your
    suits back, too, those dark
    carcasses hung in your closet, and the black
    noses of your shoes with their large pores?
15 She had taught us to take it, to hate you and take it
    until we pricked with her for your
    annihilation, Father. Now I
    pass the bums in doorways, the white
    slugs of their bodies gleaming through slits in their
20 suits of compressed silt, the stained
    flippers of their hands, the underwater
    fire of their eyes, ships gone down with the
    lanterns lit, and I wonder who took it and
    took it from them in silence until they had
25 given it all away and had nothing
    left but this.

---

[1] When Richard Nixon resigned the U.S. presidency on August 8, 1974, his exit from the
White House (by helicopter from the lawn) was televised live.

Wilfred Owen, 1893–1918

Dulce et Decorum Est[1] (1920)

Bent double, like old beggars under sacks,
Knock-kneed, coughing like hags, we cursed through sludge,
Till on the haunting flares we turned our backs
And towards our distant rest began to trudge.
5 Men marched asleep. Many had lost their boots
But limped on, blood-shod. All went lame; all blind;
Drunk with fatigue; deaf even to the hoots
Of tired, outstripped Five-Nines[2] that dropped behind.

Gas! Gas! Quick, boys!—An ecstasy of fumbling,
10 Fitting the clumsy helmets just in time;
But someone still was yelling out and stumbling
And flound'ring like a man in fire or lime . . .
Dim, through the misty panes and thick green light,
As under a green sea, I saw him drowning.
15 In all my dreams, before my helpless sight,
He plunges at me, guttering, choking, drowning.

If in some smothering dreams you too could pace
Behind the wagon that we flung him in,
And watch the white eyes writhing in his face,
20 His hanging face, like a devil's sick of sin;
If you could hear, at every jolt, the blood
Come gargling from the froth-corrupted lungs,
Obscene as cancer, bitter as the cud
Of vile, incurable sores on innocent tongues,—
25 My friend, you would not tell with such high zest
To children ardent for some desperate glory,
The old Lie: Dulce et decorum est
Pro patria mori.

[1] The title and last lines are from Horace, Odes III, ii: "Sweet and fitting it is to die for one's country."
[2] Shells that explode on impact and release poison gas.

Linda Pastan, 1932–

Ethics (1980)

In ethics class so many years ago
our teacher asked this question every fall:
if there were a fire in a museum
which would you save, a Rembrandt painting
5   or an old woman who hadn't many
years left anyhow? Restless on hard chairs
caring little for pictures or old age
we'd opt one year for life, the next for art
and always half-heartedly. Sometimes
10 the woman borrowed my grandmother's face
leaving her usual kitchen to wander
some drafty, half imagined museum.
One year, feeling clever, I replied
why not let the woman decide herself?
15 Linda, the teacher would report, eschews
the burdens of responsibility.
This fall in a real museum I stand
before a real Rembrandt, old woman,
or nearly so, myself. The colors
20 within this frame are darker than autumn,
darker even than winter—the browns of earth,
though earth's most radiant elements burn
through the canvas. I know now that woman
and painting and season are almost one
25 and all beyond saving by children.

Linda Pastan, 1932–

Marks (1978)

My husband gives me an A
for last night's supper,
an incomplete for my ironing,
a B plus in bed.
5 My son says I am average,
an average mother, but if
I put my mind to it
I could improve.
My daughter believes
10 in Pass/Fail and tells me
I pass. Wait 'til they learn
I'm dropping out.

Dorothy Parker, 1893–1967

One Perfect Rose (1937)

A single flow'r he sent me, since we met.
    All tenderly his messenger he chose;
Deep-hearted, pure, with scented dew still wet—
    One perfect rose.

5 I knew the language of the floweret;
    "My fragile leaves," it said, "his heart enclose."
Love long has taken for his amulet
    One perfect rose.

Why is it no one ever sent me yet
10   One perfect limousine, do you suppose?
Ah no, it's always just my luck to get
    One perfect rose.

Marge Piercy, 1934—

The Secretary Chant (1973)

My hips are a desk.
From my ears hang
chains of paper clips.
Rubber bands form my hair.
5 My breasts are wells of mimeograph ink.
My feet bear casters.
Buzz. Click.
My head is a badly organized file.
My head is a switchboard
10 where crossed lines crackle.
Press my fingers
and in my eyes appear
credit and debit.
Zing. Tinkle.
15 My navel is a reject button.
From my mouth issue canceled reams.
Swollen, heavy, rectangular
I am about to be delivered
of a baby
20 Xerox machine.
File me under W
because I wonce
was
a woman.

Sylvia Plath, 1932–1963

Metaphors (1960)

I'm a riddle in nine syllables,
An elephant, a ponderous house,
A melon strolling on two tendrils.
O red fruit, ivory, fine timbers!
5 This loaf's big with its yeasty rising.
Money's new-minted in this fat purse.
I'm a means, a stage, a cow in calf.
I've eaten a bag of green apples,
Boarded the train there's no getting off.

Sylvia Plath, 1932–1963

Daddy (1965)

You do not do, you do not do
Any more, black shoe
In which I have lived like a foot
For thirty years, poor and white,
5 Barely daring to breathe or Achoo.

Daddy, I have had to kill you.
You died before I had time—
Marble-heavy, a bag full of God,
Ghastly statue with one grey toe
10 Big as a Frisco seal

And a head in the freakish Atlantic
Where it pours bean green over blue
In the waters off beautiful Nauset.
I used to pray to recover you.
15 Ach, du.[1]

---

[1] Ah, you (German).

In the German tongue, in the Polish town[2]
Scraped flat by the roller
Of wars, wars, wars.
But the name of the town is common.
20 My Polack friend

Says there are a dozen or two.
So I never could tell where you
Put your foot, your root,
I never could talk to you.
25 The tongue stuck in my jaw.

It stuck in a barb wire snare.
Ich, ich, ich, ich,[3]
I could hardly speak.
I thought every German was you.
30 And the language obscene

An engine, an engine
Chuffing me off like a Jew.
A Jew to Dachau, Auschwitz, Belsen.[4]
I began to talk like a Jew.
35 I think I may well be a Jew.

The snows of the Tyrol, the clear beer of Vienna
Are not very pure or true.
With my gypsy ancestress and my weird luck
And my Taroc pack and my Taroc pack
40 I may be a bit of a Jew.

I have always been scared of *you,*
With your Luftwaffe,[5] your gobbledygoo.
And your neat moustache
And your Aryan eye, bright blue.
45 Panzer[6]-man, panzer-man, O You—

Not God but a swastika
So black no sky could squeak through.
Every woman adores a Fascist,
The boot in the face, the brute
50 Brute heart of a brute like you.

---

[2] Grabôw, where Plath's father was born.
[3] I, I, I, I (German).
[4] Nazi concentration camps.
[5] The German air force.
[6] Protected by armor. The Panzer division was the German armored division.

You stand at the blackboard, daddy,
In the picture I have of you,
A cleft in your chin instead of your foot
But no less a devil for that, no not
55 Any less the black man who

Bit my pretty red heart in two.
I was ten when they buried you.
At twenty I tried to die
And get back, back, back to you.
60 I thought even the bones would do.

But they pulled me out of the sack,
And they stuck me together with glue.
And then I knew what to do.
I made a model of you,
65 A man in black with a Meinkampf[7] look

And a love of the rack and the screw.
And I said I do, I do.
So daddy, I'm finally through.
The black telephone's off at the root,
70 The voices just can't worm through.

If I've killed one man, I've killed two—
The vampire who said he was you
And drank my blood for a year,
Seven years, if you want to know.
75 Daddy, you can lie back now.

There's a stake in your fat black heart
And the villagers never liked you.
They are dancing and stamping on you.
They always *knew* it was you.
80 Daddy, daddy, you bastard, I'm through.

[7] *Mein Kampf* (My Struggle) is Adolf Hitler's autobiography.

Edgar Allan Poe, 1809–1849

The Raven (1844)

Once upon a midnight dreary, while I pondered, weak and weary,
Over many a quaint and curious volume of forgotten lore,
While I nodded, nearly napping, suddenly there came a tapping,
As of some one gently rapping, rapping at my chamber door.
5 "'Tis some visitor," I muttered, "tapping at my chamber door—
        Only this, and nothing more."

Ah, distinctly I remember it was in the bleak December,
And each separate dying ember wrought its ghost upon the floor.
Eagerly I wished the morrow;—vainly I had sought to borrow
10 From my books surcease of sorrow—sorrow for the lost Lenore—
For the rare and radiant maiden whom the angels name Lenore—
        Nameless here for evermore.

And the silken sad uncertain rustling of each purple curtain
Thrilled me—filled me with fantastic terrors never felt before;
15 So that now, to still the beating of my heart, I stood repeating
"'Tis some visitor entreating entrance at my chamber door;—
        This it is, and nothing more."

Presently my soul grew stronger; hesitating then no longer,
"Sir," said I, "or Madam, truly your forgiveness I implore;
20 But the fact is I was napping, and so gently you came rapping,
And so faintly you came tapping, tapping at my chamber door,
That I scarce was sure I heard you"—here I opened wide the door;—
        Darkness there, and nothing more.

Deep into that darkness peering, long I stood there wondering, fearing,
25 Doubting, dreaming dreams no mortal ever dared to dream before;
But the silence was unbroken, and the darkness gave no token,
And the only word there spoken was the whispered word, "Lenore!"
This I whispered, and an echo murmured back the word, "Lenore!"—
        Merely this, and nothing more.

30 Back into the chamber turning, all my soul within me burning,
Soon I heard again a tapping somewhat louder than before.
"Surely," said I, "surely that is something at my window lattice;
Let me see, then, what thereat is, and this mystery explore—
Let my heart be still a moment and this mystery explore;—
35   'Tis the wind and nothing more!"

Open here I flung the shutter, when, with many a flirt and flutter,
In there stepped a stately raven of the saintly days of yore;
Not the least obeisance made he; not an instant stopped or stayed he;
But, with mien of lord or lady, perched above my chamber door—
40 Perched upon a bust of Pallas[1] just above my chamber door—
    Perched, and sat, and nothing more.

Then this ebony bird beguiling my sad fancy into smiling,
By the grave and stern decorum of the countenance it wore,
"Though thy crest be shorn and shaven, thou," I said, "art sure no craven,
45 Ghastly grim and ancient raven wandering from the Nightly shore—
Tell me what thy lordly name is on the Night's Plutonian shore!"
    Quoth the raven, "Nevermore."

Much I marvelled this ungainly fowl to hear discourse so plainly,
Though its answer little meaning—little relevancy bore,
50 For we cannot help agreeing that no living human being
Ever yet was blessed with seeing bird above his chamber door—
Bird or beast upon the sculptured bust above his chamber door,
    With such name as "Nevermore."

But the raven, sitting lonely on the placid bust, spoke only
55 That one word, as if his soul in that one word he did outpour.
Nothing farther then he uttered—not a feather then he fluttered—
Till I scarcely more than muttered "Other friends have flown before—
On the morrow *he* will leave me, as my hopes have flown before."
    Then the bird said "Nevermore."

60 Startled at the stillness broken by reply so aptly spoken,
"Doubtless," said I, "what it utters is its only stock and store
Caught from some unhappy master whom unmerciful Disaster
Followed fast and followed faster till his songs one burden bore—
Till the dirges of his Hope that melancholy burden bore
65   Of 'Never—nevermore.'"

But the raven still beguiling all my sad soul into smiling,
Straight I wheeled a cushioned seat in front of bird and bust and door;
Then, upon the velvet sinking, I betook myself to linking
Fancy unto fancy, thinking what this ominous bird of yore—
70 What this grim, ungainly, ghastly, gaunt, and ominous bird of yore
    Meant in croaking "Nevermore."

[1] Athena, the Greek goddess of wisdom.

This I sat engaged in guessing, but no syllable expressing
To the fowl whose fiery eyes now burned into my bosom's core;
This and more I sat divining, with my head at ease reclining
75 On the cushion's velvet lining that the lamplight gloated o'er,
But whose velvet violet lining with the lamplight gloating o'er,
She shall press, ah, nevermore!

Then, methought, the air grew denser, perfumed from an unseen censer
Swung by angels whose faint foot-falls tinkled on the tufted floor.
80 "Wretch," I cried, "thy God hath lent thee—by these angels he hath sent thee
Respite—respite and nepenthe[2] from thy memories of Lenore!
Quaff, oh quaff this kind nepenthe and forget this lost Lenore!"
Quoth the raven, "Nevermore."

"Prophet!" said I, "thing of evil!—prophet still, if bird or devil!—
85 Whether Tempter sent, or whether tempest tossed thee here ashore,
Desolate, yet all undaunted, on this desert land enchanted—
On this home by Horror haunted—tell me truly, I implore—
Is there—*is* there balm in Gilead?[3]—tell me—tell me, I implore!"
Quoth the raven, "Nevermore."

90 "Prophet!" said I, "thing of evil—prophet still, if bird or devil!
by that Heaven that bends above us—by that God we both adore—
Tell this soul with sorrow laden if, within the distant Aidenn,
It shall clasp a sainted maiden whom the angels name Lenore—
Clasp a rare and radiant maiden whom the angels name Lenore."
95   Quoth the raven, "Nevermore."

"Be that word our sign of parting, bird or fiend!" I shrieked upstarting—
"Get thee back into the tempest and the Night's Plutonian shore!
Leave no black plume as a token of that lie thy soul hath spoken!
Leave my loneliness unbroken!—quit the bust above my door!
100 Take thy beak from out my heart, and take thy form from off my door!"
Quoth the raven, "Nevermore."

And the raven, never flitting, still is sitting, still is sitting
On the pallid bust of Pallas just above my chamber door;
And his eyes have all the seeming of a demon's that is dreaming,
105 And the lamp-light o'er him streaming throws his shadow on the floor;
And my soul from out that shadow that lies floating on the floor
Shall be lifted—nevermore!

---

[2] A drug reputed by the Greeks to cause forgetfulness of sorrow.
[3] Cf. Jeremiah 8:22.

Alexander Pope, 1688–1744

Epigram. Engraved on the Collar of a Dog Which I Gave to His Royal Highness (1738 [1737])

I am his Highness' dog at Kew:[1]
Pray tell me sir, whose dog are you?

Ezra Pound, 1885–1972

The River-Merchant's Wife: A Letter[1] (1515)

While my hair was still cut straight across my forehead
I played about the front gate, pulling flowers.
You came by on bamboo stilts, playing horse,
You walked about my seat, playing with blue plums.
5 And we went on living in the village of Chokan:[2]
Two small people, without dislike or suspicion.
At fourteen I married My Lord you.
I never laughed, being bashful.
Lowering my head, I looked at the wall.
10 Called to, a thousand times, I never looked back.

[1] One of the royal palaces, near London.
[1] This is one of the many translations Pound made of Chinese poems. The poem is a free translation of Li Po's (701–762) "Two Letters from Chang-Kan."
[2] Chang-Kan.

At fifteen I stopped scowling,
I desired my dust to be mingled with yours
Forever and forever and forever.
Why should I climb the lookout?
15   At sixteen you departed,
You went into far Ku-to-yen,[3] by the river of swirling eddies,
And you have been gone five months.
The monkeys make sorrowful noise overhead.

You dragged your feet when you went out.
20   By the gate now, the moss is grown, the different mosses,
Too deep to clear them away!
The leaves fall early this autumn, in wind.
The paired butterflies are already yellow with August
Over the grass in the West garden;
25   They hurt me. I grow older.
If you are coming down through the narrows of the river Kiang,[4]
Please let me know beforehand,
And I will come out to meet you
        As far as Cho-fu-sa.[5]

Ezra Pound, 1885–1972

In a Station of the Metro (1916)

The apparition of these faces in the crowd;
Petals on a wet, black bough.

---

[3] An island in the river Ch'ū-t'ang.
[4] The Japanese name for the river Ch'ū-t'ang (see note 3). Pound's translations are based on commentaries derived from Japanese scholars; therefore, he usually uses Japanese instead of Chinese names.
[5] A beach several hundred miles upstream of Nanking.

Dudley Randall, 1914–

Ballad of Birmingham (1969)

(On the bombing of a church in Birmingham, Alabama, 1963)

"Mother dear, may I go downtown
Instead of out to play,
And march the streets of Birmingham
In a Freedom March today?"

5 "No, baby, no, you may not go,
For the dogs are fierce and wild,
And clubs and hoses, guns and jails
Aren't good for a little child."

"But, mother, I won't be alone.
10 Other children will go with me,
And march the streets of Birmingham
To make our country free."

"No, baby, no, you may not go,
For I fear those guns will fire.
15 But you may go to church instead
And sing in the children's choir."

She has combed and brushed her night-dark hair,
And bathed rose petal sweet,
And drawn white gloves on her small brown hands,
20 And white shoes on her feet.

The mother smiled to know her child
Was in the sacred place,
But that smile was the last smile
To come upon her face.

25 For when she heard the explosion,
Her eyes grew wet and wild.
She raced through the streets of Birmingham
Calling for her child.

She clawed through bits of glass and brick,
30 Then lifted out a shoe.
"O, here's the shoe my baby wore,
But, baby, where are you?"

John Crowe Ransom, 1888–1974

Bells for John Whiteside's Daughter (1924)

There was such speed in her little body,
And such lightness in her footfall,
It is no wonder her brown study
Astonishes us all.

5 Her wars were bruited in our high window.
We looked among orchard trees and beyond,
Where she took arms against her shadow,
Or harried unto the pond

The lazy geese, like a snow cloud
10 Dripping their snow on the green grass,
Tricking and stopping, sleepy and proud,
Who cried in goose, Alas,

For the tireless heart within the little
Lady with rod that made them rise
15 From their noon apple-dreams, and scuttle
Goose-fashion under the skies!

But now go the bells, and we are ready;
In one house we are sternly stopped
To say we are vexed at her brown study,
20 Lying so primly propped.

Henry Reed, 1914—

Naming of Parts (1946)

Today we have naming of parts. Yesterday,
We had daily cleaning. And tomorrow morning,
We shall have what to do after firing. But today,
Today we have naming of parts. Japonica[1]
5 Glistens like coral in all of the neighboring gardens,
     And today we have naming of parts.

This is the lower sling swivel. And this
Is the upper sling swivel, whose use you will see,
When you are given your slings. And this is the piling swivel,
10 Which in your case you have not got. The branches
Hold in the gardens their silent, eloquent gestures,
     Which in our case we have not got.

This is the safety-catch, which is always released
With an easy flick of the thumb. And please do not let me
15 See anyone using his finger. You can do it quite easy
If you have any strength in your thumb. The blossoms
Are fragile and motionless, never letting anyone see
     Any of them using their finger.

And this you can see is the bolt. The purpose of this
Is to open the breech, as you see. We can slide it
20 Rapidly backwards and forwards: we call this
Easing the spring. And rapidly backwards and forwards
The early bees are assaulting and fumbling the flowers:
     They call it easing the Spring.

They call it easing the Spring: it is perfectly easy
25 If you have any strength in your thumb: like the bolt,
And the breech, and the cocking-piece, and the point of balance,
Which in our case we have not got; and the almond-blossom
Silent in all of the gardens and the bees going backwards and forwards,
     For today we have the naming of parts.

[1]A shrub having waxy flowers in a variety of colors.

Adrienne Rich, 1929–

Living in Sin (1955)

She had thought the studio would keep itself,
no dust upon the furniture of love.
Half heresy, to wish the taps less vocal,
the panes relieved of grime. A plate of pears,
5 a piano with a Persian shawl, a cat
stalking the picturesque amusing mouse
had risen at his urging.
Not that at five each separate stair would writhe
under the milkman's tramp; that morning light
10 so coldly would delineate the scraps
of last night's cheese and three sepulchral bottles;
that on the kitchen shelf among the saucers
a pair of beetle-eyes would fix her own—
envoy from some black village in the mouldings . . .
15 Meanwhile, he, with a yawn,
sounded a dozen notes upon the keyboard,
declared it out of tune, shrugged at the mirror,
rubbed at his beard, went out for cigarettes;
while she, jeered by the minor demons,
20 pulled back the sheets and made the bed and found
a towel to dust the table-top,
and let the coffee-pot boil over on the stove.
By evening she was back in love again,
though not so wholly but throughout the night
25 she woke sometimes to feel the daylight coming
like a relentless milkman up the stairs.

Adrienne Rich, 1929–

Aunt Jennifer's Tigers (1951)

Aunt Jennifer's tigers prance across a screen,
Bright topaz denizens of a world of green.
They do not fear the men beneath the tree;
They pace in sleek chivalric certainty.

5 Aunt Jennifer's fingers fluttering through her wool
Find even the ivory needle hard to pull.
The massive weight of Uncle's wedding band
Sits heavily upon Aunt Jennifer's hand.

When Aunt is dead, her terrified hands will lie
10 Still ringed with ordeals she was mastered by.
The tigers in the panel that she made
Will go on prancing, proud and unafraid.

Adrienne Rich, 1929–

Diving into the Wreck (1973)

First having read the book of myths,
and loaded the camera,
and checked the edge of the knife-blade,
I put on
5 the body-armor of black rubber
the absurd flippers
the grave and awkward mask.
I am having to do this
not like Cousteau with his
10 assiduous team
aboard the sun-flooded schooner
but here alone.

There is a ladder.
The ladder is always there
15 hanging innocently
close to the side of the schooner.
We know what it is for,
we who have used it.
Otherwise
20 it's a piece of maritime floss
some sundry equipment.

I go down.
Rung after rung and still
the oxygen immerses me
25 the blue light
the clear atoms
of our human air.
I go down.
My flippers cripple me,
30 I crawl like an insect down the ladder
and there is no one
to tell me when the ocean
will begin.

First the air is blue and then
35 it is bluer and then green and then
black I am blacking out and yet
my mask is powerful
it pumps my blood with power
the sea is another story
40 the sea is not a question of power
I have to learn alone
to turn my body without force
in the deep element.

And now: it is easy to forget
45 what I came for
among so many who have always
lived here
swaying their crenellated fans
between the reefs
50 and besides
you breathe differently down here.

I came to explore the wreck.
The words are purposes.
The words are maps.

55 I came to see the damage that was done
and the treasures that prevail.
I stroke the beam of my lamp
slowly along the flank
of something more permanent
60 than fish or weed

the thing I came for:
the wreck and not the story of the wreck
the thing itself and not the myth
the drowned face always staring
65 toward the sun
the evidence of damage
worn by salt and sway into this threadbare beauty
the ribs of the disaster
curving their assertion
70 among the tentative haunters.

This is the place.
And I am here, the mermaid whose dark hair
streams black, the merman in his armored body
We circle silently
75 about the wreck
we dive into the hold.
I am she: I am he

whose drowned face sleeps with open eyes
whose breasts still bear the stress
80 whose silver, copper, vermeil cargo lies
obscurely inside barrels
half-wedged and left to rot
we are the half-destroyed instruments
that once held to a course
85 the water-eaten log
the fouled compass

We are, I am, you are
by cowardice or courage
the one who finds our way
90 back to this scene
carrying a knife, a camera
a book of myths
in which
our names do not appear.

Edwin Arlington Robinson, 1869–1935

Mr. Flood's Party (1921)

Old Eben Flood, climbing alone one night
Over the hill between the town below
And the forsaken upland hermitage
That held as much as he should ever know
5 On earth again of home, paused warily.
The road was his with not a native near;
And Eben, having leisure, said aloud,
For no man else in Tilbury Town to hear:

"Well, Mr. Flood, we have the harvest moon
10 Again, and we may not have many more;
The bird is on the wing, the poet[1] says,
And you and I have said it here before.
Drink to the bird." He raised up to the light
The jug that he had gone so far to fill,
15 And answered huskily: "Well, Mr. Flood,
Since you propose it, I believe I will."

Alone, as if enduring to the end
A valiant armor of scarred hopes outworn,
He stood there in the middle of the road
20 Like Roland's ghost winding a silent horn.[2]
Below him, in the town among the trees,
Where friends of other days had honored him,
A phantom salutation of the dead
Rang thinly till old Eben's eyes were dim.

25 Then, as a mother lays her sleeping child
Down tenderly, fearing it may awake,
He set the jug down slowly at his feet
With trembling care, knowing that most things break;
And only when assured that on firm earth
30 It stood, as the uncertain lives of men
Assuredly did not, he paced away,
And with his hand extended paused again:

[1] Edward FitzGerald and Omar Khayyám.
[2] In the *Chanson de Roland,* a medieval French romance, Roland and his soldiers are trapped and killed at a mountain pass; Roland waits until the last minute before his death to sound his horn to signal for help from his emperor, Charlemagne.

"Well, Mr. Flood, we have not met like this
In a long time; and many a change has come
35 To both of us, I fear, since last it was
We had a drop together. Welcome home!"
Convivially returning with himself,
Again he raised the jug up to the light;
And with an acquiescent quaver said:
40 "Well, Mr. Flood, if you insist, I might.

"Only a very little, Mr. Flood—
For auld lang syne. No more, sir; that will do."
So, for the time, apparently it did,
And Eben evidently thought so too;
45 For soon amid the silver loneliness
Of night he lifted up his voice and sang,
Secure, with only two moons listening,
Until the whole harmonious landscape rang—

"For auld lang syne." The weary throat gave out,
50 The last word wavered; and the song being done,
He raised again the jug regretfully
And shook his head, and was again alone.
There was not much that was ahead of him,
And there was nothing in the town below—
55 Where strangers would have shut the many doors
That many friends had opened long ago.

Edwin Arlington Robinson, 1869–1935

Richard Cory (1897)

Whenever Richard Cory went down town,
We people on the pavement looked at him:
He was a gentleman from sole to crown,
Clean favored, and imperially slim.

5 And he was always quietly arrayed,
And he was always human when he talked;
But still he fluttered pulses when he said,
"Good-morning," and he glittered when he walked.

And he was rich—yes, richer than a king—
10 And admirably schooled in every grace:
In fine, we thought that he was everything
To make us wish that we were in his place.

So on we worked, and waited for the light,
And went without the meat, and cursed the bread;
15 And Richard Cory, one calm summer night,
Went home and put a bullet through his head.

Theodore Roethke, 1908–1963

My Papa's Waltz (1948)

The wiskey on your breath
Could make a small boy dizzy;
But I hung on like death:
Such waltzing was not easy.

5 We romped until the pans
Slid from the kitchen shelf;
My mother's countenance
Could not unfrown itself.

The hand that held my wrist
10 Was battered on one knuckle;
At every step you missed
My right ear scraped a buckle.

You beat time on my head
With a palm caked hard by dirt,
15 Then waltzed me off to bed
Still clinging to your shirt.

Theodore Roethke, 1908–1963

I Knew a Woman (1958)

I knew a woman, lovely in her bones,
When small birds sighed, she would sigh back at them;
Ah, when she moved, she moved more ways than one:
The shapes a bright container can contain!
5 Of her choice virtues only gods should speak,
Or English poets who grew up on Greek
(I'd have them sing in chorus, cheek to cheek).

How well her wishes went! She stroked my chin,
She taught me Turn, and Counter-turn, and Stand;
10 She taught me Touch, that undulant white skin;
I nibbled meekly from her proffered hand;
She was the sickle; I, poor I, the rake,
Coming behind her for her pretty sake
(But what prodigious mowing we did make).

15 Love likes a gander, and adores a goose:
Her full lips pursed, the errant note to seize;
She played it quick, she played it light and loose;
My eyes, they dazzled at her flowing knees;
Her several parts could keep a pure repose,
20 Or one hip quiver with a mobile nose
(She moved in circles, and those circles moved).

Let seed be grass, and grass turn into hay:
I'm martyr to a motion not my own;
What's freedom for? To know eternity.
25 I swear she cast a shadow white as stone.
But who would count eternity in days?
These old bones live to learn her wanton ways:
(I measure time by how a body sways).

Christina Rossetti, 1830–1894

Uphill (1861)

Does the road wind uphill all the way?
    Yes, to the very end.
Will the day's journey take the whole long day?
    From morn to night, my friend.

5 But is there for the night a resting-place?
    A roof for when the slow dark hours begin.
May not the darkness hide it from my face?
    You cannot miss that inn.

Shall I meet other wayfarers at night?
10   Those who have gone before.
Then must I knock, or call when just in sight?
    They will not keep you standing at that door.

Shall I find comfort, travel-sore and weak?
    Of labor you shall find the sum.
15 Will there be beds for me and all who seek?
    Yea, beds for all who come.

Anne Sexton, 1928–1974

Her Kind (1960)

I have gone out, a possessed witch,
haunting the black air, braver at night;
dreaming evil, I have done my hitch
over the plain houses, light by light:
5 lonely thing, twelve-fingered, out of mind.
A woman like that is not a woman, quite.
I have been her kind.

I have found the warm caves in the woods,
filled them with skillets, carvings, shelves,
10 closets, silks, innumerable goods;
fixed the suppers for the worms and the elves:
whining, rearranging the disaligned.
A woman like that is misunderstood.
I have been her kind.

15 I have ridden in your cart, driver,
waved my nude arms at villages going by,
learning the last bright routes, survivor
where your flames still bite my thigh
and my ribs crack where your wheels wind.
20 A woman like that is not ashamed to die.
I have been her kind.

William Shakespeare, 1564–1616

My Mistress' Eyes Are Nothing Like the Sun (1609)

My mistress' eyes are nothing like the sun;
Coral is far more red than her lips' red;
If snow be white, why then her breasts are dun;
If hairs be wires, black wires grow on her head.
5 I have seen roses damasked red and white,
But no such roses see I in her cheeks;
And in some perfumes is there more delight
Than in the breath that from my mistress reeks.
I love to hear her speak, yet well I know
10 That music hath a far more pleasing sound;
I grant I never saw a goddess go:
My mistress, when she walks, treads on the ground.
   And yet, by heaven, I think my love as rare
   As any she, belied with false compare.

William Shakespeare, 1564–1616

Let Me Not to the Marriage of True Minds (1609)

Let me not to the marriage of true minds
Admit impediments.[1] Love is not love
Which alters when it alteration finds,
Or bends with the remover to remove:
5 Oh, no! it is an ever-fixéd mark,
That looks on tempests and is never shaken;
It is the star to every wandering bark,
Whose worth's unknown, although his height[2] be taken.
Love's not Time's fool,[3] though rosy lips and cheeks
10 Within his bending sickle's compass come;
Love alters not with his brief hours and weeks,
But bears it out even to the edge of doom.[4]
If this be error and upon me proved,
I never writ, nor no man ever loved.

---

[1] A reference to "The Order of Solemnization of Matrimony" in the Anglican Book of Common Prayer: "I require that if either of you know any impediments why ye may not be lawfully joined together in Matrimony, ye do now confess it."
[2] Although the altitude of a star may be measured, its worth is unknowable.
[3] That is, mocked by Time.
[4] Doomsday.

William Shakespeare, 1564–1616

Not Marble, Nor the Gilded Monuments (1609)

Not marble, nor the gilded monuments
Of princes, shall outlive this powerful rhyme;
But you shall shine more bright in these contents
Than unswept stone, besmeared with sluttish time.
5 When wasteful war shall statues overturn,
And broils root out the work of masonry,
Nor Mars[1] his sword nor war's quick fire shall burn
The living record of your memory.
'Gainst death and all-oblivious enmity
10 Shall you pace forth; your praise shall still find room
Even in the eyes of all posterity
That wear this world out to the ending doom.
So, till the judgment that yourself arise,
You live in this, and dwell in lovers' eyes.

William Shakespeare, 1564–1616

When, in Disgrace with Fortune and Men's Eyes (1609)

When, in disgrace with Fortune and men's eyes,
I all alone beweep my outcast state,
And trouble deaf heaven with my bootless[1] cries,
And look upon myself and curse my fate,
5 Wishing me like to one more rich in hope,
Featured like him, like him with friends possessed,

[1] God of War.
[1] Futile.

Desiring this man's art, and that man's scope,
With what I most enjoy contented least,
Yet in these thoughts myself almost despising,
10 Haply[2] I think on thee, and then my state,
Like to the lark at break of day arising
From sullen earth, sings hymns at heaven's gate;
    For thy sweet love rememb'red such wealth brings
    That then I scorn to change my state with kings.

Percy Bysshe Shelley, 1792–1822

Ozymandias[1] (1818)

I met a traveler from an antique land
Who said: Two vast and trunkless legs of stone
Stand in the desert. Near them, on the sand,
Half sunk, a shattered visage lies, whose frown,
5 And wrinkled lip, and sneer of cold command,
Tell that its sculptor well those passions read
Which yet survive, stamped on these lifeless things,
The hand that mocked them, and the heart that fed;
And on the pedestal these words appear:
10 "My name is Ozymandias, king of kings:
Look on my works, ye Mighty, and despair!"
Nothing beside remains. Round the decay
Of that colossal wreck, boundless and bare
The lone and level sands stretch far away.

[2] Luckily.
[1] The Greek name for Ramses II, ruler of Egypt in the thirteenth century B.C.

Leslie Marmon Silko, 1948–

Where Mountain Lion Lay Down with Deer (1973)

I climb the black rock mountain
  stepping from day to day
                silently.
I smell the wind for my ancestors
5   pale blue leaves
    crushed wild mountain smell.
Returning
  up the gray stone cliff
  where I descended
10   a thousand years ago.
Returning to faded black stone.
  where mountain lion lay down with deer.
It is better to stay up here
                watching wind's reflection
15   in tall yellow flowers.
The old ones who remember me are gone
          the old songs are all forgotten
and the story of my birth.
How I danced in snow-frost moonlight
20   distant stars to the end of the Earth,
How I swam away
            in freezing mountain water
            narrow mossy canyon tumbling down
                out of the mountain
25   out of the deep canyon stone
              down
                the memory
                    spilling out
                    into the world.

Cathy Song, 1955—

Lost Sister (1983)

1
In China,
even the peasants
named their first daughters
Jade—
5 the stone that in the far fields
could moisten the dry season,
could make men move mountains
for the healing green of the inner hills
glistening like slices of winter melon.

10 And the daughters were grateful:
they never left home.
To move freely was a luxury
stolen from them at birth.
Instead, they gathered patience,
15 learning to walk in shoes
the size of teacups,[1]
without breaking—
the arc of their movements
as dormant as the rooted willow,
20 as redundant as the farmyard hens.
But they traveled far
in surviving,
learning to stretch the family rice,
to quiet the demons,
25 the noisy stomachs.

[1] A reference to the practice of binding young girls' feet so that they remain small. This practice, which crippled women, was common in China until the communist revolution.

2
There is a sister
across the ocean,
who relinquished her name,
diluting jade green
30 with the blue of the Pacific.
Rising with a tide of locusts,
she swarmed with others
to inundate another shore.
In America,
35 there are many roads
and women can stride along with men.

But in another wilderness,
the possibilities,
the loneliness,
40 can strangulate like jungle vines.
The meager provisions and sentiments
of once belonging—
fermented roots, Mah-Jongg[2] tiles and firecrackers—
set but a flimsy household
45 in a forest of nightless cities.
A giant snake rattles above,
spewing black clouds into your kitchen.
Dough-faced landlords
slip in and out of your keyholes,
50 making claims you don't understand,
tapping into your communication systems
of laundry lines and restaurant chains.

You find you need China:
your one fragile identification,
55 a jade link
handcuffed to your wrist.
You remember your mother
who walked for centuries,
footless—
60 and like her,
you have left no footprints,
but only because
there is an ocean in between,
the unremitting space of your rebellion.

---

[2] Or mahjong, an ancient Chinese game played with dice and tiles.

William Stafford, 1914–1993

Traveling Through the Dark (1962)

Traveling through the dark I found a deer
dead on the edge of the Wilson River road.
It is usually best to roll them into the canyon:
that road is narrow; to swerve might make more dead.

5 By glow of the tail-light I stumbled back of the car
and stood by the heap, a doe, a recent killing;
she had stiffened already, almost cold.
I dragged her off; she was large in the belly.

My fingers touching her side brought me the reason—
10 her side was warm; her fawn lay there waiting,
alive, still, never to be born.
Beside that mountain road I hesitated.

The car aimed ahead its lowered parking lights;
under the hood purred the steady engine.
15 I stood in the glare of the warm exhaust turning red;
around our group I could hear the wilderness listen.

I thought hard for us all—my only swerving—
then pushed her over the edge into the river.

Wallace Stevens, 1879–1955

The Emperor of Ice-Cream (1923)

Call the roller of big cigars,
The muscular one, and bid him whip
In kitchen cups concupiscent curds.
Let the wenches dawdle in such dress
5 As they are used to wear, and let the boys
Bring flowers in last month's newspapers.
Let be be the finale of seem.
The only emperor is the emperor of ice-cream.

Take from the dresser of deal,[1]
10 Lacking the three glass knobs, that sheet
On which she embroidered fantails[2] once
And spread it so as to cover her face.
If her horny feet protrude, they come
To show how cold she is, and dumb.
15 Let the lamp affix its beam.
The only emperor is the emperor of ice-cream.

[1] Fir or pine wood.
[2] According to Stevens, "the word fantails does not mean fans, but fantail pigeons."

Jonathan Swift, 1667–1745

A Description of the Morning (1709)

Now hardly here and there a hackney-coach[1]
Appearing, showed the ruddy morn's approach.
Now Betty[2] from her master's bed had flown,
And softly stole to discompose her own.
5 The slip shod 'prentice from his master's door
Had pared the dirt, and sprinkled round the floor.
Now Moll had whirled her mop with dext'rous airs,
Prepared to scrub the entry and the stairs.
The youth with broomy stumps began to trace
10 The kennel-edge[3] where wheels had worn the place.
The small-coal man[4] was heard with cadence deep,
Till drowned in shriller notes of chimney-sweep:
Duns[5] at his lordship's gate began to meet;
And brick-dust Moll had screamed through half the street.[6]
15 The turnkey now his flock returning sees,
Duly let out a-nights to steal for fees.[7]
The watchful bailiffs take their silent stands,[8]
And schoolboys lag with satchels in their hands.

---

[1] Hired coach. *Hardly:* scarcely; i.e., they are just beginning to appear.
[2] A stock name for a servant girl. Moll (lines 7, 14) is a frequent lower-class nickname.
[3] Edge of the gutter that ran down the middle of the street. *Trace:* "To find old Nails" (Swift's note).
[4] A seller of coal and charcoal.
[5] Bill collectors.
[6] Selling powdered brick that was used to clean knives.
[7] Jailers collected fees from prisoners for their keep and often let them out at night so they could steal to pay expenses.
[8] Looking for those on their "wanted" lists.

Alfred, Lord Tennyson, 1809–1892

Ulysses[1] (1833)

It little profits that an idle king,
By this still hearth, among these barren crags,
Matched with an agèd wife, I mete and dole
Unequal laws unto a savage race
5 That hoard, and sleep, and feed, and know not me.
I cannot rest from travel; I will drink
Life to the lees. All times I have enjoyed
Greatly, have suffered greatly, both with those
That loved me, and alone; on shore, and when
10 Through scudding drifts the rainy Hyades[2]
Vexed the dim sea. I am become a name;
For always roaming with a hungry heart
Much have I seen and known—cities of men
And manners, climates, councils, governments,
15 Myself not least, but honored of them all—
And drunk delight of battle with my peers,
Far on the ringing plains of windy Troy.[3]
I am a part of all that I have met;
Yet all experience is an arch wherethrough
20 Gleams that untraveled world whose margin fades
Forever and forever when I move.
How dull it is to pause, to make an end,
To rust unburnished, not to shine in use!
As though to breathe were life! Life piled on life
25 Were all too little, and of one to me
Little remains; but every hour is saved
From that eternal silence, something more,
A bringer of new things; and vile it were
For some three suns to store and hoard myself,
30 And this grey spirit yearning in desire

---

[1] A legendary Greek king of Ithaca and hero of Homer"s *Odyssey,* Ulysses (or Odysseus) is noted for his daring and cunning. After his many adventures—including encounters with the Cyclops, the cannibalistic Laestrygones, and the enchantress Circe—Ulysses returned home to his faithful wife, Penelope. Tennyson portrays an older Ulysses pondering his situation.
[2] A group of stars whose rising was supposedly followed by rain, and hence stormy seas.
[3] An ancient city in Asia Minor. According to legend, Paris, King of Troy, abducted Helen, initiating the famed Trojan war, in which numerous Greek heroes, including Ulysses, fought.

To follow knowledge like a sinking star,
Beyond the utmost bound of human thought.
    This is my son, mine own Telemachus,
To whom I leave the scepter and the isle—
35 Well-loved of me, discerning to fulfill
This labor, by slow prudence to make mild
A rugged people, and through soft degrees
Subdue them to the useful and the good.
Most blameless is he, centered in the sphere
40 Of common duties, decent not to fail
In offices of tenderness, and pay
Meet adoration to my household gods,
When I am gone. He works his work, I mine.
    There lies the port; the vessel puffs her sail;
45 There gloom the dark, broad seas. My mariners,
Souls that have toiled, and wrought, and thought with me—
That ever with a frolic welcome took
The thunder and the sunshine, and opposed
Free hearts, free foreheads—you and I are old;
50 Old age hath yet his honor and his toil.
Death closes all; but something ere the end,
Some work of noble note, may yet be done,
Not unbecoming men that strove with Gods.
The lights begin to twinkle from the rocks;
55 The long day wanes; the low moon climbs; the deep
Moans round with many voices. Come, my friends,
'Tis not too late to seek a newer world.
Push off, and sitting well in order smite
The sounding furrows; for my purpose holds
60 To sail beyond the sunset, and the baths
Of all the western stars, until I die.
It may be that the gulfs will wash us down;
It may be we shall touch the Happy Isles,[4]
And see the great Achilles,[5] whom we knew.
65 Though much is taken, much abides; and though
We are not now that strength which in old days
Moved earth and heaven, that which we are, we are—
One equal temper of heroic hearts,
Made weak by time and fate, but strong in will
70 To strive, to seek, to find, and not to yield.

[4] Elysium, or Paradise, believed to be in the far western ocean.
[5] Famed Greek hero of the Trojan War.

Dylan Thomas, 1914–1953

Do Not Go Gentle into That Good Night[1] (1952)

Do not go gentle into that good night,
Old age should burn and rave at close of day;
Rage, rage against the dying of the light.

Though wise men at their end know dark is right,
5 Because their words had forked no lightning they
Do not go gentle into that good night.

Good men, the last wave by, crying how bright
Their frail deeds might have danced in a green bay,
Rage, rage against the dying of the light.

10 Wild men who caught and sang the sun in flight,
And learn, too late, they grieved it on its way,
Do not go gentle into that good night.

Grave men, near death, who see with blinding sight
Blind eyes could blaze like meteors and be gay,
15 Rage, rage against the dying of the light.

And you, my father, there on the sad height,
Curse, bless, me now with your fierce tears, I pray,
Do not go gentle into that good night.
Rage, rage against the dying of the light.

[1] This poem was written during the last illness of the poet's father, D. J. Thomas.

Jean Toomer, 1894–1967

Reapers (1923)

Black reapers with the sound of steel on stones
Are sharpening scythes. I see them place the hones
In their hip-pockets as a thing that's done,
And start their silent swinging, one by one.
5 Black horses drive a mower through the weeds,
And there, a field rat, startled, squealing bleeds,
His belly close to ground. I see the blade,
Blood-stained, continue cutting weeds and shade.

Edmund Waller, 1606–1687

Go, Lovely Rose (1645)

Go, lovely rose,
Tell her that wastes her time and me
That now she knows,
When I resemble her to thee,
5 How sweet and fair she seems to be.

Tell her that's young
And shuns to have her graces spied,
That hadst thou sprung
In deserts where no men abide,
10 Thou must have uncommended died.

Small is the worth
Of beauty from the light retired:
Bid her come forth,
Suffer herself to be desired,
15 And not blush so to be admired.

Then die, that she
The common fate of all things rare
May read in thee,
How small a part of time they share
20 That are so wondrous sweet and fair.

Walt Whitman, 1819–1892

A Noiseless Patient Spider (1881)

A noiseless patient spider,
I mark'd where on a little promontory it stood isolated,
Mark'd how to explore the vacant vast surrounding,
It launch'd forth filament, filament, filament, out of itself,
5 Ever unreeling them, ever tirelessly speeding them.

And you O my soul where you stand,
Surrounded, detached, in measureless oceans of space,
Ceaselessly musing, venturing, throwing, seeking the spheres to
    connect them,
Till the bridge you will need be form'd, till the ductile anchor hold,
10 Till the gossamer thread you fling catch somewhere, O my soul.

Walt Whitman, 1819–1892

Cavalry Crossing a Ford (1865)

A line in long array where they wind betwixt green islands,
They take a serpentine course, their arms flash in the sun—hark to
    the musical clank,
Behold the silvery river, in it the splashing horses loitering stop to
    drink,
Behold the brown-faced men, each group, each person a picture, the
    negligent rest on the saddles,
5 Some emerge on the opposite bank, others are just entering the ford
    while,
Scarlet and blue and snowy white,
The guidon flags flutter gayly in the wind.

Walt Whitman, 1819–1892

When I Heard the Learn'd Astronomer (1865)

When I heard the learn'd astronomer,
When the proofs, the figures, were ranged in columns before me,
When I was shown the charts and diagrams, to add, divide, and
    measure them,
5 When I sitting heard the astronomer where he lectured with much
    applause in the lecture-room,
How soon unaccountable I became tired and sick,
Till rising and gliding out I wander'd off by myself,
In the mystical moist night-air, and from time to time,
10 Look'd up in perfect silence at the stars.

Richard Wilbur, 1921–

Love Calls Us to the Things of This World[1] (1956)

    The eyes open to a cry of pulleys,[2]
And spirited from sleep, the astounded soul
Hangs for a moment bodiless and simple
As false dawn.
5   Outside the open window
The morning air is all awash with angels.

---

[1] A phrase from St. Augustine's *Commentary on the Psalms.*
[2] Laundry pulleys, designed so that clothes can be hung on the line inside and then sent out-
doors to dry.

Some are in bed-sheets, some are in blouses,
Some are in smocks: but truly there they are.
Now they are rising together in calm swells
10 Of halcyon³ feeling, filling whatever they wear
With the deep joy of their impersonal breathing;
    Now they are flying in place,⁴ conveying
The terrible speed of their omnipresence, moving
And staying like white water; and now of a sudden
15 They swoon down into so rapt a quiet
That nobody seems to be there.
                                    The soul shrinks

    From all that it is about to remember,
From the punctual rape of every blessèd day,
20 And cries,
            "Oh, let there be nothing on earth but laundry,
Nothing but rosy hands in the rising steam
And clear dances done in the sight of heaven."
    Yet, as the sun acknowledges
25 With a warm look the world's hunks and colors,
The soul descends once more in bitter love
To accept the waking body, saying now
In a changed voice as the man yawns and rises,

        "Bring them down from their ruddy gallows;
30 Let there be clean linen for the backs of thieves;
Let lovers go fresh and sweet to be undone,
And the heaviest nuns walk in a pure floating
Of dark habits,
                keeping their difficult balance."

³ Serene.
⁴ Like planes in a formation.

William Carlos Williams, 1883–1963

Red Wheelbarrow (1923)

so much depends
upon

a red wheel
barrow

glazed with rain
water

beside the white
chickens

William Carlos Williams, 1883–1963

The Dance (1944)

In Brueghel's great picture, The Kermess,[1]
the dancers go round, they go round and
around, the squeal and the blare and the
tweedle of bagpipes, a bugle and fiddles
5 tipping their bellies (round as the thick-
sided glasses whose wash they impound)
their hips and their bellies off balance
to turn them. Kicking and rolling about
the Fair Grounds, swinging their butts, those
10 shanks must be sound to bear up under such
rollicking measures, prance as they dance
in Brueghel's great picture, The Kermess.

[1] Painting by Peter Brueghel the elder (ca. 1525–1569).

William Wordsworth, 1770–1850

The World Is Too Much with Us (1807)

The world is too much with us; late and soon,
Getting and spending, we lay waste our powers;
Little we see in Nature that is ours;
We have given our hearts away, a sordid boon!
5 This Sea that bares her bosom to the moon;
The winds that will be howling at all hours,
And are up-gathered now like sleeping flowers;
For this, for everything, we are out of tune;
It moves us not. Great God! I'd rather be
10 A Pagan suckled in a creed outworn;
So might I, standing on this pleasant lea,
Have glimpses that would make me less forlorn;
Have sight of Proteus[1] rising from the sea;
Or hear old Triton[2] blow his wreathèd horn.

---

[1] Sometimes said to be Poseidon's son, this Greek sea god had the ability to change shapes at will and to tell the future.
[2] The trumpeter of the sea, this sea god is usually pictured blowing on a conch shell. Triton was the son of Poseidon, ruler of the sea.

William Wordsworth, 1770–1850

I Wandered Lonely as a Cloud (1807)

I wandered lonely as a cloud
   That floats on high o'er vales and hills,
When all at once I saw a crowd,
   A host, of golden daffodils,
5 Beside the lake, beneath the trees,
Fluttering and dancing in the breeze.

Continuous as the stars that shine
   And twinkle on the milky way,
They stretched in never-ending line
10   Along the margin of a bay:
Ten thousand saw I at a glance,
Tossing their heads in sprightly dance.

The waves beside them danced; but they
   Out-did the sparkling waves in glee;
15 A poet could not but be gay,
   In such a jocund company;
I gazed—and gazed—but little thought
What wealth the show to me had brought:

For oft, when on my couch I lie
20   In vacant or in pensive mood,
They flash upon that inward eye
   Which is the bliss of solitude;
And then my heart with pleasure fills,
And dances with the daffodils.

James Wright, 1927–1980

A Blessing (1961)

Just off the highway to Rochester, Minnesota,
Twilight bounds softly forth on the grass.
And the eyes of those two Indian ponies
Darken with kindness.
5 They have come gladly out of the willows
To welcome my friend and me.
We step over the barbed wire into the pasture
Where they have been grazing all day, alone.
They ripple tensely, they can hardly contain their happiness
10 That we have come.
They bow shyly as wet swans. They love each other.
There is no loneliness like theirs.
At home once more,
They begin munching the young tufts of spring in the darkness.
15 I would like to hold the slenderer one in my arms,
For she has walked over to me
And nuzzled my left hand.
She is black and white,
Her mane falls wild on her forehead,
20 And the light breeze moves me to caress her long ear
That is delicate as the skin over a girl's wrist.
Suddenly I realize
That if I stepped out of my body I would break
Into blossom.

William Butler Yeats, 1865–1939

Leda and the Swan (1924)

A sudden blow: the great wings beating still
Above the staggering girl, her thighs caressed
By the dark webs, her nape caught in his bill,
He holds her helpless breast upon his breast.

5 How can those terrified vague fingers push
The feathered glory from her loosening thighs?
And how can body, laid in that white rush,
But feel the strange heart beating where it lies?

A shudder in the loins engenders there
10 The broken wall, the burning roof and tower
And Agamemnon dead.
                    Being so caught up,
So mastered by the brute blood of the air,
Did she put on his knowledge with his power
Before the indifferent beak could let her drop?

William Butler Yeats, 1865–1939

Sailing to Byzantium (1927)

That is no country for old men. The young
In one another's arms, birds in the trees
—Those dying generations—at their song,
The salmon-falls, the mackerel-crowded seas,
5 Fish, flesh, or fowl, commend all summer long
Whatever is begotten, born, and dies.
Caught in that sensual music all neglect
Monuments of unaging intellect.

An aged man is but a paltry thing,
10 A tattered coat upon a stick, unless
Soul clap its hands and sing, and louder sing
For every tatter in its mortal dress,
Nor is there singing school but studying
Monuments of its own magnificence;
15 And therefore I have sailed the seas and come
To the holy city of Byzantium.

O sages standing in God's holy fire
As in the gold mosaic of a wall,
Come from the holy fire, perne in a gyre,
20 And be the singing-masters of my soul.
Consume my heart away; sick with desire
And fastened to a dying animal
It knows not what it is; and gather me
Into the artifice of eternity.

25 Once out of nature I shall never take
My bodily form from any natural thing,
But such a form as Grecian goldsmiths make
Of hammered gold and gold enameling
To keep a drowsy Emperor awake;
30 Or set upon a golden bough to sing
To lords and ladies of Byzantium
Of what is past, or passing, or to come.

William Butler Yeats, 1865–1939

The Second Coming[1] (1921)

Turning and turning in the widening gyre[2]
The falcon cannot hear the falconer;
Things fall apart; the center cannot hold;
Mere anarchy is loosed upon the world,
5   The blood-dimmed tide is loosed, and everywhere
The ceremony of innocence is drowned;
The best lack all conviction, while the worst
Are full of passionate intensity.[3]

Surely some revelation is at hand;
10   Surely the Second Coming is at hand;
The Second Coming! Hardly are those words out
When a vast image out of *Spiritus Mundi*[4]
Troubles my sight: somewhere in sands of the desert
A shape with lion body and the head of a man,
15   A gaze blank and pitiless as the sun,
Is moving its slow thighs, while all about it
Reel shadows of the indignant desert birds.
The darkness drops again; but now I know
That twenty centuries[5] of stony sleep
20   Were vexed to nightmare by a rocking cradle,
And what rough beast, its hour come round at last,
Slouches towards Bethlehem to be born?

[1] The Second Coming usually refers to the return of Christ. Yeats theorized cycles of history much like the turning of a wheel. Here he offers a poetic comment on his view of the dissolution of civilization at the end of one such cycle.
[2] Spiral.
[3] Lines 4–8 refer to the Russian Revolution (1917).
[4] The Spirit of the World. Yeats believed all souls to be connected by a "Great Memory."
[5] The centuries since the birth of Christ.

Credits

W. H. Auden, "Musee Des Beaux Arts," from *W. H. Auden: Collected Poems* by W. H. Auden. Copyright © 1940 and renewed 1968 by W. H. Auden. Reprinted by permission of Random House, Inc.

Margaret Atwood, "You Fit Into Me," from *Power Politics* by Margaret Atwood. Reprinted with permission of Stoddart Publishing Company.

Elizabeth Bishop, "The Fish," from *The Complete Poems* by Elizabeth Bishop. Copyright © 1940, 1956, 1979 by Elizabeth Bishop. Copyright © 1979, 1983 by Alice Helen Meathfessel. Reprinted by permission of Farrar, Straus, & Giroux, Inc.

Gwendolyn Brooks, "The Bean Eaters," and "We Real Cool," from *Blacks* by Gwendolyn Brooks. Copyright © 1991 by Gwendolyn Brooks. Published by Third World Press, Chicago, 1991.

Lucille Clifton, "Homage to My Hips," from *Two-Headed Woman* by Lucille Clifton. Reprinted by permission of Curtis Brown Ltd. Copyright © 1980 by University of Massachusetts Press. First appeared in *Two-Headed Woman.* Published by University of Massachusetts Press.

Countee Cullen, "For A Lady I Know," Reprinted by permission of GRM Associates, Inc., Agents for the Estate of Ida M. Cullen. From *On These I Stand* by Countee Cullen. Copyright © 1925 by Harper & Brothers, copyright renewed 1953 by Ida M. Cullen.

E. E. Cummings, "in Just-," and "Buffalo Bill's," are reprinted from *Complete Poems: 1904-1962* by E. E. Cummings, Edited by George J. Firmage, by permission of Liveright Publishing Corporation. Copyright © 1923, 1951, 1991 by the Trustees for the E. E. Cummings Trust. Copyright © 1976 by George James Firmage.

Emily Dickinson, "I Heard a Fly Buzz—When I Died," "Because I Could not Stop for Death," "I Taste a Liquor Never Brewed," and "I Like to See it Lap the Miles," Reprinted by permission of the publishers and the Trustees of Amherst College from *The Poems of Emily Dickinson,* Thomas H.